HAIR MATTERS

HAIR MATTERS

Elayne Becker

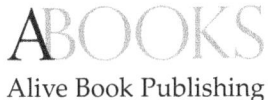

ABOOKS
Alive Book Publishing

Hair Matters
Copyright © 2016 by Elayne Becker

Additional copies may be ordered from the publisher for educational, business,
promotional or premium use. For information, contact ALIVE Book Publishing at:
alivebookpublishing.com, or call (925) 837-7303.

Cover Art by Elayne Becker
Book Design by Alex Johnson

ISBN 13
978-1-63132-032-3

ISBN 10
1-63132-032-7

Library of Congress Control Number: 2016943687

Library of Congress Cataloging-in-Publication Data is available upon request.

First Edition

Published in the United States of America by ALIVE Book Publishing
and ALIVE Publishing Group, imprints of Advanced Publishing LLC
3200 A Danville Blvd., Suite 204, Alamo, California 94507
alivebookpublishing.com

PRINTED IN THE UNITED STATES OF AMERICA

10 9 8 7 6 5 4 3 2 1

This book is a collection of stories and humorous observations meant to pay homage to the fibrous strands of protein that make up the hair on our heads. It is a personal account of a stylist and educator who came late to the profession, at age sixty two, and describes the impact hair has had in her life.

"How you look and feel connects powerfully to your hair."

Elayne Lois Becker

This book was written for the students I have
taught and loved, who inspire me everyday.
For my clients, friends and family.
And for Charlie who teaches me everyday
in every way that we matter.

TABLE OF CONTENTS

INTRODUCTION
OUR GRAND STRANDS

I have spent a lifetime looking in mirrors checking the reflection to see if every hair on my head was positioned in the right place. Similar to a drill sergeant in the army making sure every strand was obeying my orders and each hair standing exactly where it was assigned. Or like Alice, peering into the looking glass always assessing the image for any distortions that might be visible.

I have spent decades loving and hating those grand strands. What purpose did they serve and why did they deserve to have so much of my attention and money lavished on them over the years? The pages ahead attempt to answer these questions: why does our hair have the power to affect us so completely and why does it influence the way we feel and the choices we make? Everyone has a hair story to tell and share about how their hair had affected them at different times in their life. This hair retrospective presents a collection of memories and observations about hair's influence starting in the early fifties to the present decade. No matter how old we get our hair plays a significant role in our lives. Our hair matters.

Each morning we leave the warmth and comfort of our beds to face the different universes in which we rotate. Our career paths may be different from each other; yet, we all face the morning mirror with our own special routines and expectations. Our drawers and cabinets overflow with the lotions and potions we buy and apply to our face and hair. These formulations and preparations aid us in the beauty routines we perform at the start of each new day. Mine starts with a cleanser, foundation and finishes with mascara. The morning ritual awakens my tired face and I am transformed into better version of my earlier self. Years and lines have melted away temporarily and I am grateful for retinol, blush and concealers. These ceremonial practices give me the confidence I need for the challenges of the day ahead.

After applying my mascara, I am ready for the blow dry. Billions of dollars are spent every year in the hair industry on our hair. We all have our favorite combinations of hair products that we use on our hair hoping for lasting and successful results. Our hair often times can be our agony and our ecstasy. Beauty experts are trained in schools to help us perform magic on those grand strands of protein to aid and support us on our quest for the holy grail of hair perfection.

Hair has a language that speaks to us in many different ways. Hair is a representation of our ancestry and culture. Our heredity determines the texture of our hair— curly, wavy or straight. The density is also determined by our heredity, dictating how much hair we will have or will not have. Sometimes a grandfather's deep recession line at the frontal lobe can appear generations later. Our genetics is also responsible for the presence of melanin, the color pigments that are in the cortex of each hair cell. Will our hair have more of the red to yellow color pigments called phenomelanin or the darker ones eumelanin?

What we do after the distribution of our DNA depends on our own creative choices to experiment and experience. The technology today is more advanced than ever to help overcome the challenges our hair presents. There are mousses and gels to thicken our hair, color to change or enhance, perms to give our hair curl or relaxers to remove them, and products designed to free us from frizz. The corner salon or pharmacy gives us the opportunity to be as creative as we choose to be with our hair.

How we choose to style our hair can be influenced by the current popular culture, the celebrity we most admire, current magazines, movies or television. We are influenced by the hair of the celebrities, and are captured by their look and they affect the choices we make. Rhianna, Kim Kardashian, Halle Berry, Cameron Diaz, Emma Watson and Charlize Theron ignite our imagination and we then try to duplicate their hair style,cuts and color. Trying to replicate their look helps us to feel better about ourselves and helps to build our own self-esteem.

Hair can influence how we feel each day and can be a barometer of how we treat others. A 'bad hair' day can make us want to hide and not be seen. We just don't feel good on a bad hair day. Why is it that the day we decide to go out without makeup or not wash or fuss with our hair, we always bump into someone we don't want to see? Embarrassed, we prefer to hide from them in a different aisle of the grocery store, hoping they didn't see us. On a good hair day, the opposite is true. We feel wonderful and the last thing we want to do is hide. In fact the more who witness our fabulous hair day the better. Our hair matters.

A hair style can represent the flavor of decades past and thus becomes a time capsule from that era, symbolizing our own personal history. A picture from a high school yearbook has the power to trigger a long forgotten memory to make you laugh, or wistfully sigh that so much time has passed. How you looked and styled your hair can transport you back to more youthful time. A forgotten memory can be refreshed again in your mind's eye.

After a long thirty year career in interior design, hair became a vehicle for change in my life. I started cosmetology school at sixty two years of age -- I was the oldest student by at least forty years. The challenges were great, but the results were extraordinary.

Hair was not only going to be a metaphor for change in my life, it would become one of my greatest teachers. Hair taught to me love and value what is real, exposing the frailties of my humanity and linking me to my true identity. And most importantly not to let my age define me. Those amazing strands are a metaphor and symbol of my life's journey.

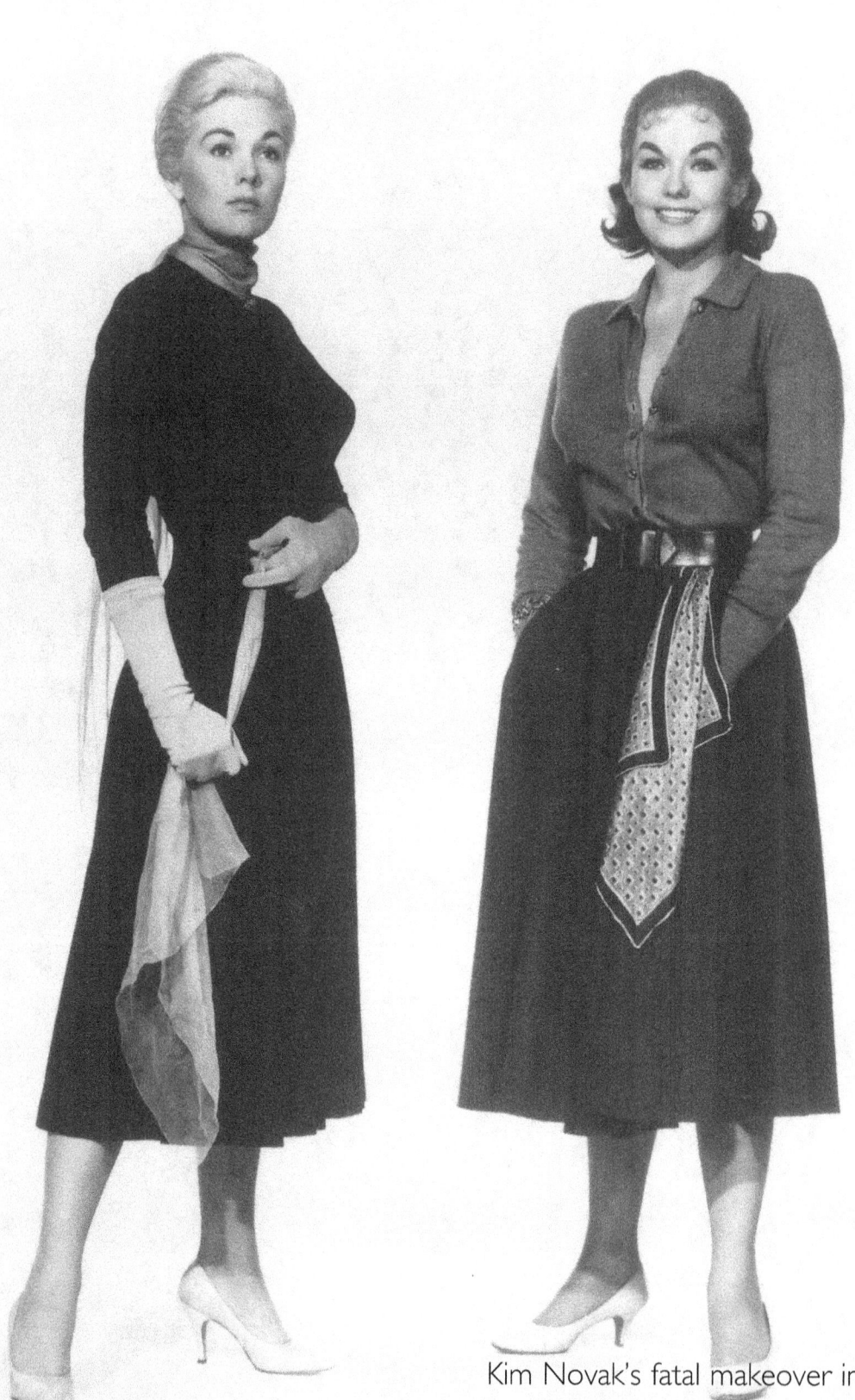

Kim Novak's fatal makeover in *Vertigo*.

CHAPTER 1
A PLACE OF THEIR OWN

"Wouldn't you like to get away?
Sometimes you want to go
Where everybody knows your name,
And they're always glad you came."
You want to be where you can see,
Our troubles are all the same
You want to be where everybody knows
Your name"

> Theme song from television show, *Cheers,* by
> Gary Portnoy and Judy Heartangelo

I was nine years old in 1955, and I remember walking into the hair salon my Aunt frequented weekly. The shop was located in Chicago between the streets of Addison and Cornelia. When I was growing up, hair salons were called beauty parlors. Walking in was my first introduction to the mysteries of women and beauty. The sights and smells permeated my psyche and the romance of those rituals and places remain with me still.

The beauty parlors from that decade were exclusive only to women; no male was seen except for an occasional stylist. My aunt's beauty parlor was called Dorothy La Doux. If you couldn't find Aunt Katie you knew exactly where you could. It seemed Dorothy La Doux was her second residence because of the long hours she spent there.

In the fifties, a hair stylist wore a crisp white dress uniform similar to the nurses of the day, the stylist's legs were encased in white nylons and white shoes, and sometimes the stylist even wore a white nurse's cap on her head. If you have seen the 1958 movie Alfred Hitchcock's *Vertigo*, Kim Novak had her fatal make over at a very posh hair salon in San Francisco. It was located inside the elegant Ransohoff's department store where the stylists were wearing the ascribed white uniforms, which denoted cleanliness and professionalism.

You knew as soon as you opened the doors to Dorothy LA Doux salon there was magic inside. The smell of the aerosol hair sprays filled the air and mingled with the fragrances of shampoo, nail polishes and polish removers. The odors were foreign and exotic and for me would always be associated with beauty.

There were long rows of dryers along the wall where women were sitting under them. Lined up in front of the seated women were manicure tables. Their hands were extended getting massaged and nails were getting polished. Tiny glass bottles were filled with shimmering colored lacquers of reds oranges and pinks all lined up on one side of the table. When polish was applied, their nails were transformed into precious jewels at the fingers tips. Fluffy white towels and small bowels of water were at the other side of each manicure table.

The ladies under the dyers had their hair wound around rollers with bright pink and powder blue, metallic hair nets tied over the rollers. Tissue was applied over their ears to protect them from the metal clips getting to hot from the heat of the dryers they were sitting under. Women were chatting with the manicurist or their eyes were closed enjoying the pampering that was taking place underneath the heat that would dry their hair on rollers locking in place their waves and curls.

Mirrored cubicles were where the hair dressers performed their services private from the rest of the salon. Women would be sitting sipping coffee and eating donuts while bleach was smeared on their hair like whip cream on pies. Aunt Katie's humorous stories made her the centerpiece of the salon, her platinum blond hair was styled in a round shape with heavy amounts of lacquer sprayed on the style she wore. Her hair was so shiny that it resembled a full moon when seen from the back.

She was meticulous about her appointments and never let a shadow of her black roots show at the base of her scalp. I believe she just liked being wrapped in the cocoon of all that was offered at her neighborhood salon.

There was a buzz of conversations, neighborhood gossip and stories were shared while the ladies were curtained and draped under the plastic capes. Tables were piled with the latest magazines of the day; *Ladies Home Journal, Mc Calls,* movie magazines, *Photo Play* and *Silver Screen.* My personal favorite was the *Saturday Evening Post,* which featured the treasured illustrations by the great artist Norman Rockwell on the covers. He would draw seasonal pictures of the lives of families done with humor and great skill.

Looking back I now understand the intimacy and comradery beauty parlors offered to the women of their day. Barbershops for men gave the same spirit to its community of men gathered together.

My mother raised her three children without the aid of modern conveniences; she never owned her own washing machine. We lived in an apartment on the top third floor of the building, and she carried babies and bags of groceries up and down those back breaking stairs several times each day. Large heavy bags swollen with laundry were also carried up and down those same arduous stairs to the basement where the washing was performed.

Sheets and towels were washed in a machine that did not rinse the clothes they had to be put separately through the wringer that would pull the clothing into a nearby sink filled with clear water to remove the soap suds. After the clothes were rinsed, the wringer would again be used to pull the excess water from articles. The basket on the cement floor was filled with the wet laundry waiting patiently for her to hang them on the overhead ropes to dry, no matter what the season. Hours would then be spent standing with a hot iron in hand removing the wrinkles from the freshly washed garments.

This process could take several days depending on the size of the family, we were five. My mother would sweat in Chicago's hot summers and freeze in Chicago's harsh winters in that cold dark basement. Dinners were always cooked from scratch with no thought of take home or take out. Dishes were washed nightly by hand, as well as the floors washed on tender knees. The women who worked outside the home had double duty. Much was asked of these women.

In hindsight I now realize the real purpose the beauty salons of my mother's day served to its neighborhood community. It was a place women could go and have a moment for themselves in a lifetime of caring for others. Once a week someone would caress and massage their hands and wash their hair. A time to have a gossip and share their hardships, unload their burdens and take a vacation from housework and raising families for just a few hours. The neighborhood salon was much more than a place to get a haircut or a manicure. It was a place to renew oneself, it was a community of women coming together and sharing fellowship. The salon was a place of importance to the neighborhood that it served.

I can't remember if any of us noticed or complimented our mother's hair when she arrived home from her weekly appointment at her hairdresser, I hope we did. I know the stairs lying quietly outside the heavy front door were less of a burden to her on those days.

Today we have sleek and modern salons and spas, corporate and individually owned. Men get their hair cut sitting next to women getting bleach and color applied on their head, both embarrassed by the shared intimacy. No one gets a manicure while sitting under a dryer any more. A woman who got a sitter for her children might be seated next to someone else's child screaming and crying while getting a haircut, imposing on her quiet moment of restoration.

I can't help feeling that something has been lost along the way. Maybe it's the absence of intimacy and privacy; or perhaps just the magic of a community of women coming together in a place of their own, the neighborhood salon.

CHAPTER 2
THE LEGEND
AND THE PONYTAIL

"Chantilly lace
And a pretty face
And a pony tail hanging down"

Written by the Big Bopper; sung by Jerry Lee Lewis

I was twelve years old in 1958 when my family moved to a new location. I had to transfer to a new school and start eighth grade at the Le Moyne School in Chicago where friendships were already formed and cemented. In those years there were no middle schools as there are now. You started Kindergarten and graduated eight years later all in the same building. By the time you matriculated from grammar school you pretty much knew everyone including all the teachers, office workers, janitors and they knew you.

Every day I felt like a stranger in my new school. I would long for the feeling of belonging to the little school that I left on Broadway and Melrose and the comfort of familiar streets, store owners, friends and neighbors.

Trying to fit in and be noticed in a new school was my full time occupation. What to wear the first day of school after summer's end was a ritual performed by most pubescent girls. The right outfit along with the right hair would set the stage in our minds for everything good that might follow; principally popularity and acceptance. A lot was at stake how you looked and the impression you would make on school's first day pecking order.

I don't remember what I wore that day, but I do remember my hair. I don't think I will ever forget my hair on my first day at my new school. I went to bed with wet hair because we didn't have hair dryers then. I carefully constructed pin curls hoping by morning my hair would be dry. At daylight those carefully-made pin curls sprang forward in an over-powering amount of frizz and waves not to mention an avalanche of uncontrollable curls. To my surprise, I went to bed dreaming that I would awaken to a smooth, sleek page boy similar to the one Marilyn Monroe wore in the movie, *How to Marry a Millionaire.*

I felt panic looking at my hair in the mirror along with a stomach aching to get rid of the breakfast it no longer wanted. A pony tail was my only solution. After all the frizz and volume, I was left with one inch of tail. Humiliation and disappointment was my entrance into eighth grade at my new school.

My most admired cousin also attended the eighth grade with me. Susie was known in my family as adorable and the possessor of beautiful hair. Not only was her hair thick and lustrous but the color was dishwater with platinum streaks made naturally by the sun. Women today would pay hundreds of dollars monthly to have Susie's highlights. Susie was also famous for her curls, hand made by her mother.

Estelle, Susie's mother, did everyone's hair in the family, acting as a practicing stylist without a license. She had the "knack" the family would say to do 'curls' and 'perms' all from her dining room on Grace Street.

The very popular girls at grammar school all had great hair. It would take me years to learn how to manage mine. Learning to reverse perm my hair with a Toni in years ahead would help in Chicago's heavy humidity. In the imminent future portable hair dryers would change everything. A plastic hood with tiny small holes would be positioned on your head, so when air was pumped into the hood, it would expand like a parachute opening. A hose would connect to a pink suitcase that supplied the hot air when it was plugged into the wall socket. It was wonderful to sit on your bed with that parachute on your head and be able to dry your hair and do your homework all at the same time. We were then free of sleeping on painful rollers, metal clips and wet hair, but that was not till high school. Meanwhile I'm still suffering with my one inch pony tail and it was my first day starting eighth grade.

If I had started my first day of school with a smooth page boy it might have changed everything. Instead I wanted to be Terry or Susie, anyone but me.

Having a great ponytail in 1958 was an insurance policy toward popularity. A very long and beautiful ponytail meant you would be admired accepted, invited to parties, and asked to dances. The eight to ten inches of hair made envy and admiration possible.

I can't remember when I first saw Karen, but I had heard about her. Everyone had. Her hair was legend. She had the longest ponytail I had ever seen. It started at her shoulders and floated down to her waist, one long curl. Karen was a pretty girl but her ponytail gave her the extra confidence that the rest of us didn't have. We -- the other girls -- would say that her hair made her and it did.

Karen went through grammar school and high school confident and admired with her pony tail swinging back and forth just like the one Jerry Lee Lewis was singing about, and we were all green with hair envy. Sometimes, Karen would wear the pony tail to one side swinging it the front of her chest and twirling the long enviable curl around her finger as she spoke. One day I believe, when Karen was a junior in high school, Karen had decided to cut her long legendary ponytail. Her hair was reduced to a shoulder-length flip some-times adorned it with colorful elastic headbands. The legend had died. Karen never looked the same; we were no longer envious of Karen, she now looked like everyone else.

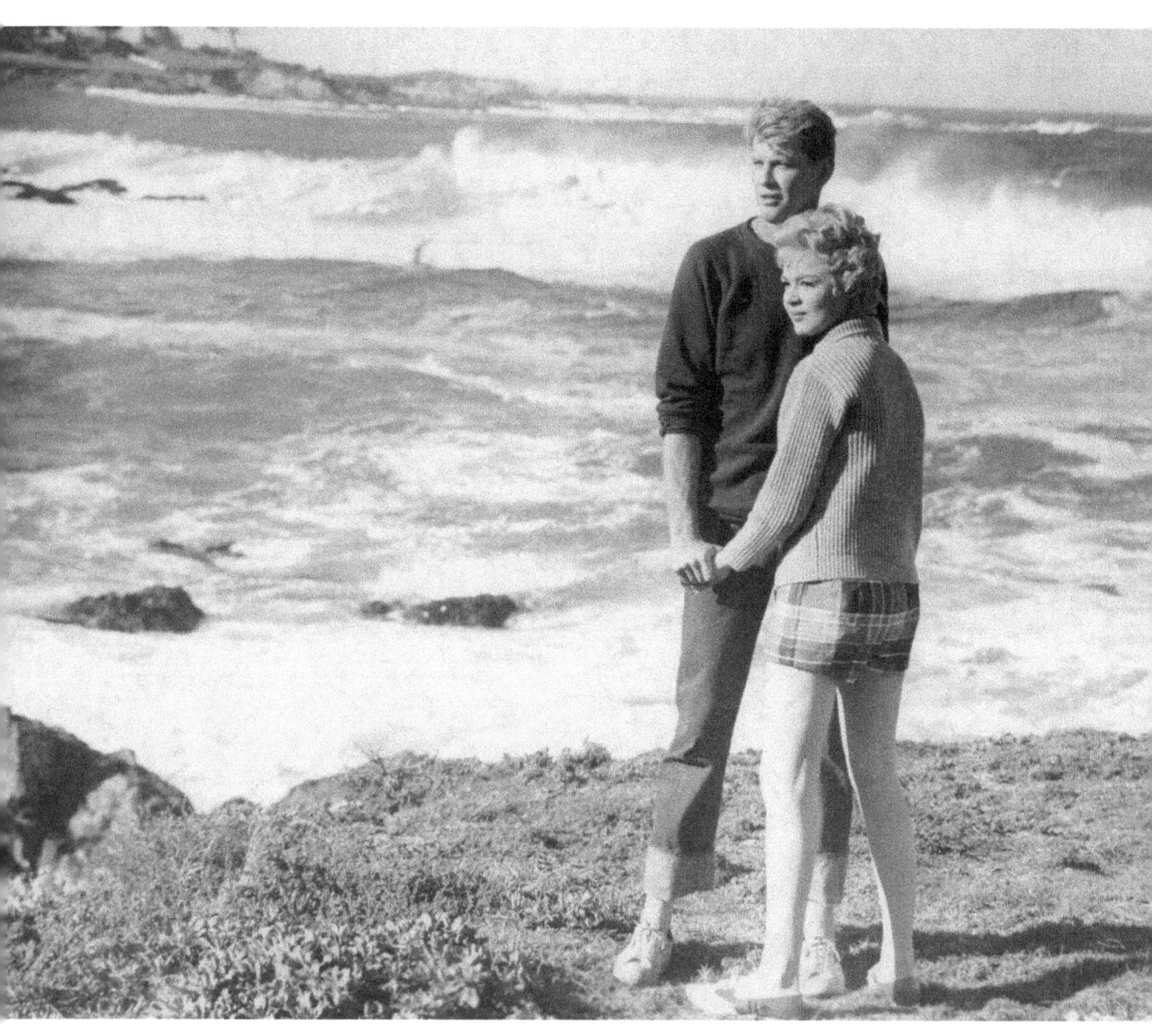

Sandra Dee and Troy Donahue in *A Summer Place*.

CHAPTER 3
REVENGE OF
THE HAIR MUMMIES

"Look at me
I'm Sandra Dee,
Lousy with Virginity,
Won't go to bed till
I'm legally wed,
I can't, I'm Sandra Dee."

From the movie, *Grease*

The musicians and screen idols of our youth are a significant part of the cherished landscape of our childhood. They grow and age with us, and become part of our own personal history. When they pass from this life, we mourn them because they were part of the decades and times we shared together.

Rizzo, played by Stockard Channing in the 1978 movie, *Grease* introduced millions of people to Sandra Dee singing that popular song. The song could never do justice to what Sandra Dee represented to girls of her generation. We all wanted look like her, talk like her, and have our hair like her. We just wanted to be Sandra Dee in every way.

Sandra Dee's hair was a short golden orb of curls that was called the 'bubble" that surrounded her adorable face. In 1959 a movie was made called a *Summer Place*. The movie represented a summer's romance and the youth

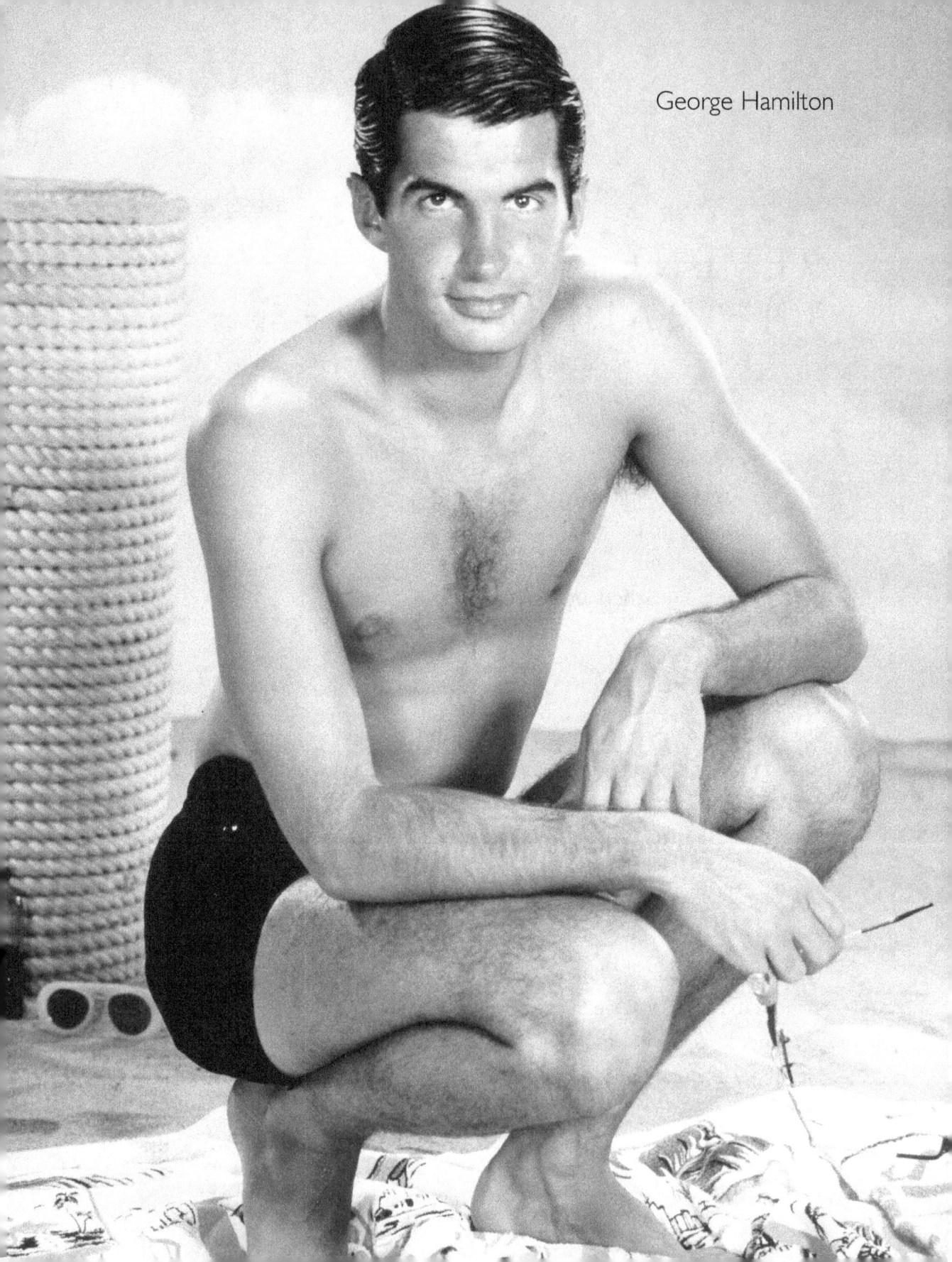

George Hamilton

and mores of the time. It spoke to us and shared our thoughts of how to be in love, have desires and still remain virginal when in college.

Troy Donahue was the perfect complement to be the male teen idol to play opposite Sandra Dee in the movie. He was a tall blond also with perfect hair and together they were hair perfection. The background music in the movie *A Summer Place* only enhanced the images of these two screen idols. Watching them in a darkened movie theater on a Saturday afternoon with your girlfriends was nothing short of magic.

The summer of 59 we dreamed our dreams listening to the theme from *A Summer Place* played by Percy Faith and his orchestra, written by Max Steiner. Waiting anxiously for WLS to play it on the radio's "top ten chart of the day."

If you get a chance to rent the movie, it's worth it. The story line may be dated; but it's a perfect time capsule of the late fifties and the values your parents or grandparents grew up with. And believe me Sandra Dee was no virgin like the one Rizzo sings about.

Watching one of the beach scenes in the movie, I suddenly realized Sandra Dee's hair never moved on that wind swept beach. In fact in any of the beach movies of the day no one's hair ever moved on a windy beach. Even the Frankie and Annette *Beach Party* movies followed the unspoken commandant, "Hair shalt not move under any weather conditions in the fifties and early sixties decades."

The best example of motionless hair in a beach movie would have to be the 1961 film *Where the Boys Are.* George Hamilton plays Ryder Smith a senior from Brown University at spring break Fort Lauderdale, Florida. His entrance in the movie begins with Ryder walking the beach extremely tanned searching for love. Soon he will meet the equally lovely Meredith, played by

Delores Hart. When the two meet Ryder then draws the iconic question mark in the sand which was a very cool and romantic way of asking Meredith her name. However, the real question of course was how did his hair not move one inch throughout the entire beach movie? It certainly followed the rule of frozen hair fashioned into a perfect sculpture of precision.

Short of cement, we sprayed and sprayed our hair until it was "stiff" and motionless with lacquer from an aerosol can so it would dare not move. After we rolled it, dried it and teased it into something resembling a lampshade, we then sprayed it over and over again. Actually it was a lampshade; we all wore lampshades on our heads.

It was a battle everyday not to have our hair move in the wind, which was really difficult, because I was living in the windiest city of all, Chicago. We wore all kinds of scarves on our heads made from silk, chiffon and cotton, and even crocheted wool, which looked like spider-webs woven together in different shapes and sizes. These were our weapons against the elements.

My arms and elbows were always raised in a permanent upward position around my head battling to keep every strand of my lampshade in place. I would walk backwards against the wind risking my life protecting my hair. In the evening we would wrap toilet paper around these coiffures to insure it would not move when we slept. My mother, my sister and I all had "toilet paper-wrapped heads" before going to bed at night; all three of us looking like the "Revenge of the Hair Mummies." I trained myself never to turn on my side when I slept. I would remain vigilant and police my hair against any movement day or night.

Soon the British were coming and I don't mean the ones with white wigs and red coats, or the ones Paul Revere was yelling about. This British import would save us from ourselves and our hair. The four new heart throbs coming to America in 1964 would change everything. Through their music and their look they would shake up our world and cause a sensation. Their hair was much longer than what most people were wearing at the time and it actually moved. This exciting new import or the lads from London called themselves the Beatles and nothing would ever be the same. Our hair was on its way to freedom.

Hair would symbolize a whole new change to our generation, and the music would lead the way. In 1965, Michelle of the Mamas and the Papas would swing her long shiny hair to the music of *California Dreaming.* Mary of Peter and Paul wore her swinging blond hair long and then added her trademark bangs. The Beach Boys were singing about the tanned and beautiful "California girls." Joan Baez would sing with her long, straight hair flowing over her shoulders and the guitar she was playing. Unlike the stiff and frozen hair of the fifties, everyone's hair was now moving gloriously. Goodbye rollers! Goodbye hair spray! Goodbye toilet paper! Goodbye scarfs! I could now turn over in bed. Hello movement. Welcome shiny, long, beautiful, straight, swinging hair.

Uh! Oh! Hello to ironing using hair relaxers, and battling the curl and the wave against the humidity of Chicago's summers. Until this time hair was frozen with hair spray. The rules were changed and we now asked our hair to swing and shine in unison just like our music. One battle was over, another now began.

Au revoir, Sandra Dee. We now wanted to look like Marianne Faithful, Michelle of the Mamas and the Papas, Mary and Joan. And all of us desperately wishing, "we were the California girls" the beach boys were singing about. Where, oh where, is the portable flatiron to make our hair quest a little easier? Not for a couple more decades.

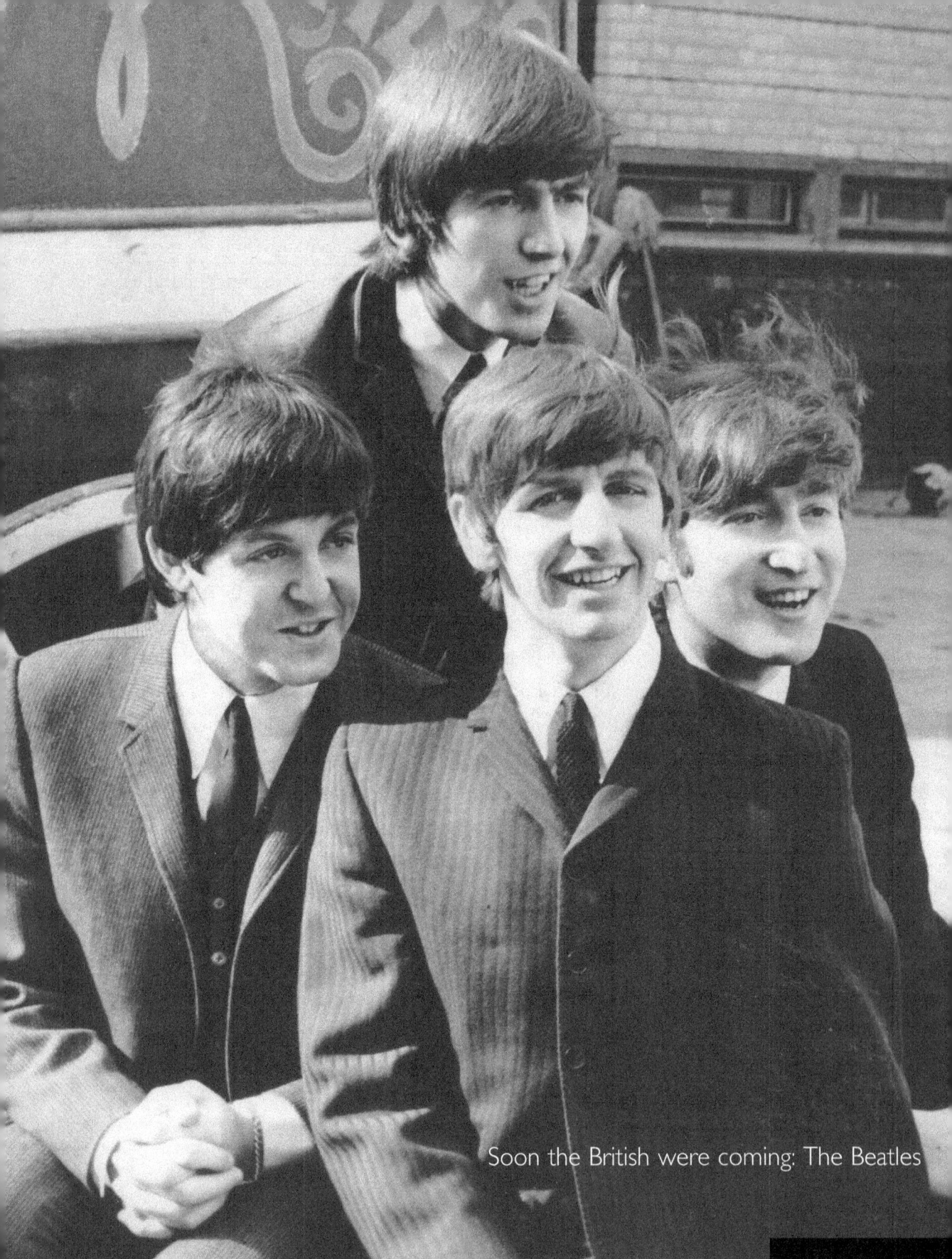

Soon the British were coming: The Beatles

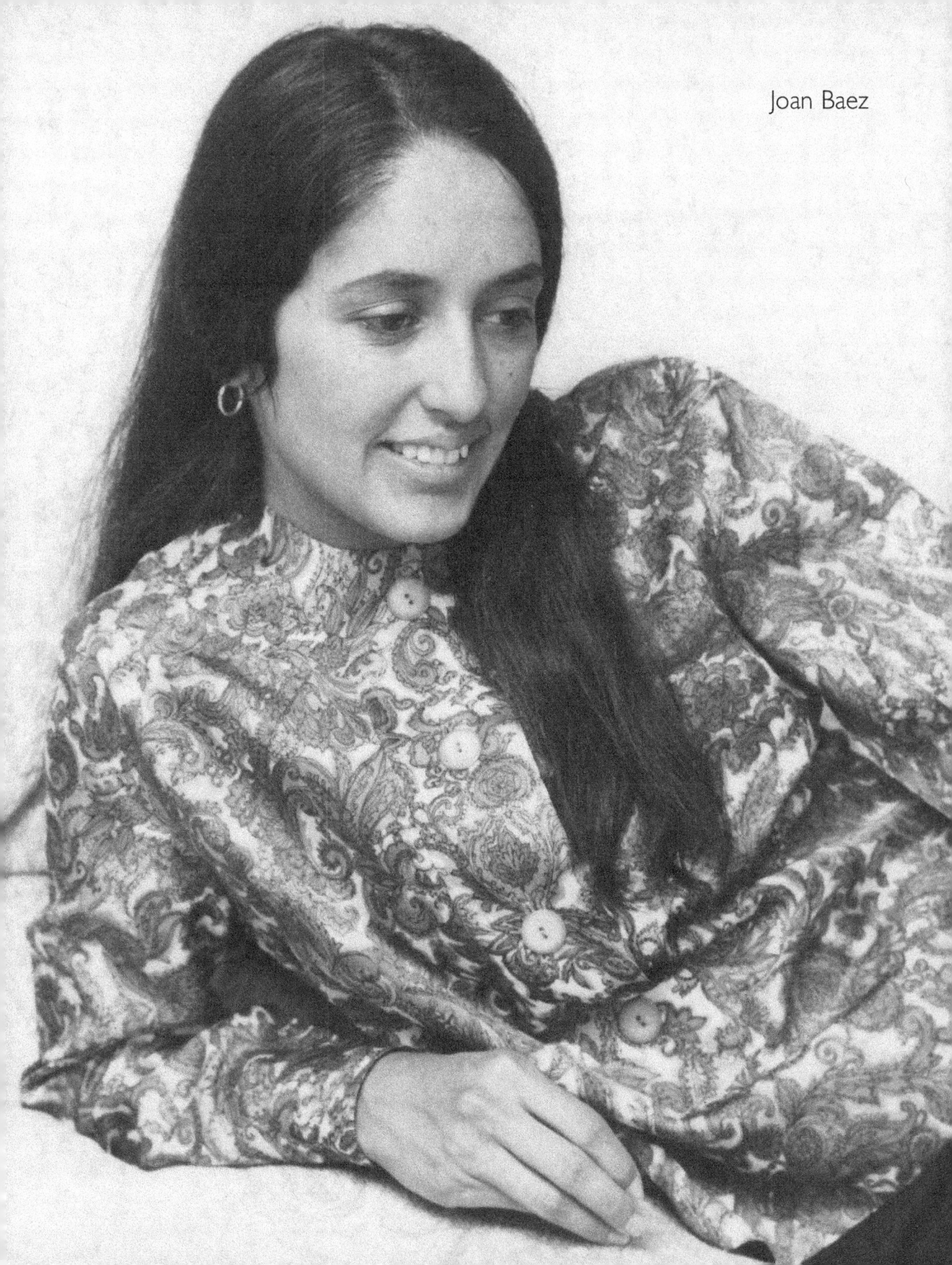

Joan Baez

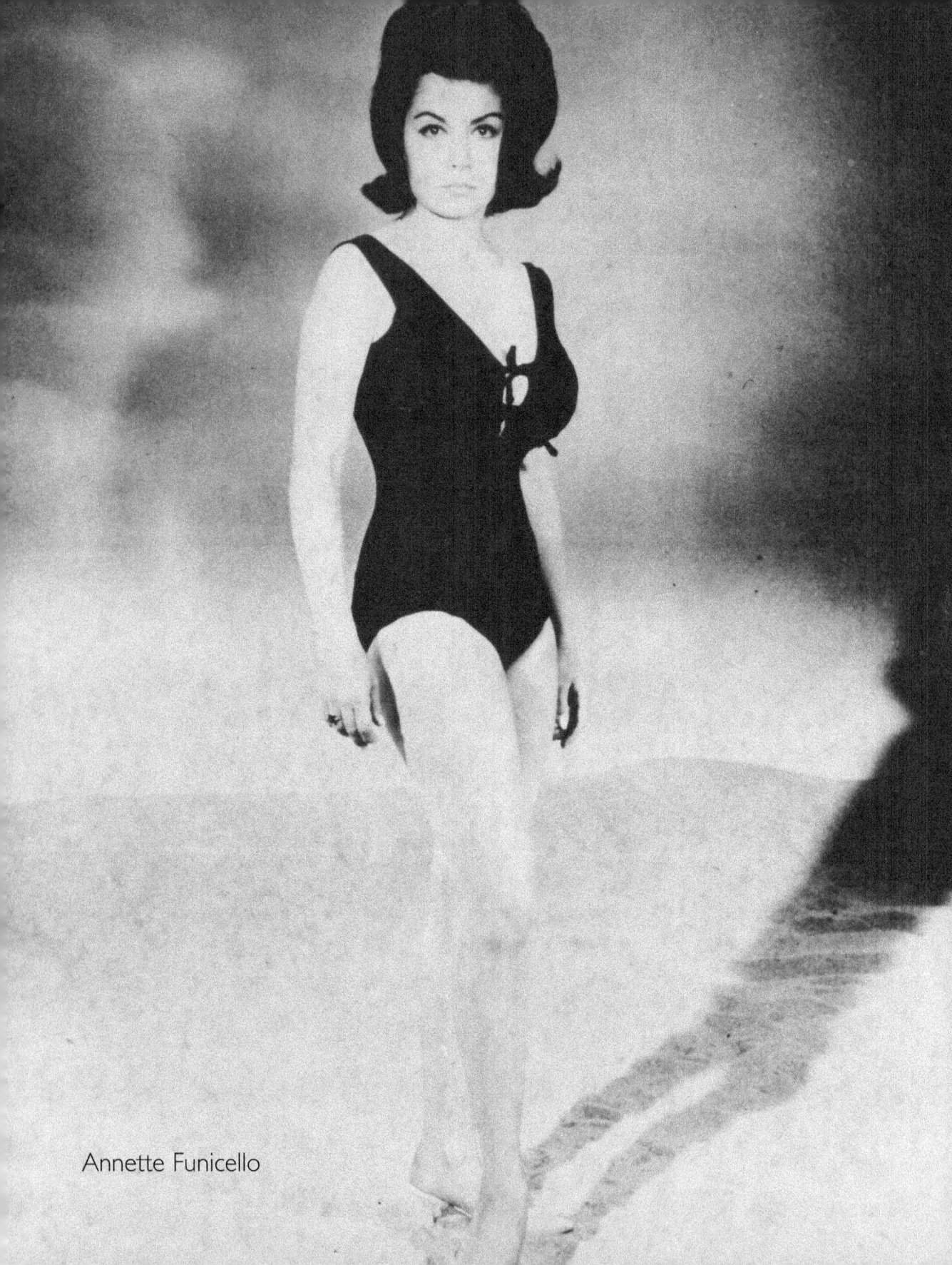

Annette Funicello

CHAPTER 4
THE SASSON

"Well she was just 17
You know what I mean
And the way she looked was way beyond compare."

McCartney/Lennon — sung by the Beatles

Years later when I was an educator at a cosmetology school; I leisurely walked to the various areas where guests and students were stationed working on clients. It was the latter part of the day and leaving the job to go home was quickly approaching.

What caught my eye and caused me to stop and chat with a guest was a picture of a haircut that the client sitting in the chair was hoping to duplicate. The picture was Vidal Sasson's delicious 'five point' haircut. Known in the sixties as "the Sasson" it was worn by hundreds of knowing and stylish women of that era, and principally Mary Quant, a fashion icon

Almost five decades later, a young woman was enamored with that same style. I stopped and chatted with the student and the client about the haircut and reminisced with them about my first experience with it. I'm afraid I was not able to explain sufficiently the emotional impact that the Sassoon haircut had on me when I was a senior at Lakeview High School in Chicago 1963.

The photograph of that haircut triggered a memory that was forgotten and hidden from my consciousness. Recalling the moment was tinged with sadness, realizing that so much time had passed since I was a senior in Lakeview High School. It was surprising that fifty years later that awe still lay buried and was still as fresh and alive as it was yesterday: a memory waiting patiently to be remembered.

The beautiful girls of high school would wield their power over us. What they wore, how they looked and how they acted would capture and hold our hearts and imaginations. They would always be a measure or standard-bearer of our own self esteem.

We would be enamored by their style until a new celebrity would come along and add to our own insignificance. Maybe, if we had become conscious of our own gifts we would have been free of the hold they had on our esteem. Time would eventually release us from their images and our feelings of inferiority. Although we would always be curious about what life had brought to the beautiful and popular girls, and we secretly hoped they were struggling just a little as we once had.

Pat was a senior class mate of mine in high school. Pat was a pretty girl; yet, walking the halls of our high school, she would have gone unnoticed. Taller than most, height was not a virtue then. The boys of high school were much shorter than the girls; most had not reached full maturation so all the smaller, cuter girls won the hearts of most of the young men. This was before the age of super models.

Pat wore glasses, clear at the lower half, solid at the top, kind of nerdy even then. The early sixties fashion was 'big' hair, the kind that expanded, Annette Funicello hair, teased and fashioned into a lacquered balloons. We all sported large hair balloons on our heads. We teased the hair and then sculptured them into geometric shapes. Sometimes we added a small bow made of ribbon or a plastic-colored barrette worn at the side of our balloon. We would also put that same small bow at the center of the bangs we wore, similar to the way the French poodles were accessorized at the time.

I was not a big fan of Pat because my very best friend at the time was now becoming best friends with Pat and I was jealous. Best friends were territorial and 'best friend' stealers were considered predators. I was careful and cool with Pat.

There was a very famous hairdresser who had his salon on the expensive and exclusive Michigan Avenue in Chicago. Anyone who had the money could make appointments with him. I had heard about him but I still went to my mother's neighborhood salon whose stylist knew nothing of the new emerging haircuts and styles.

Shocked was the word when Pat revealed she had made an appointment with Mr. Famous. How did she know about him and then take two, maybe even three, buses to downtown Chicago for her appointment?

Pat had worn her very large hair long to her shoulders. A Sasson haircut was small and the hair was cut above the ear, exposing both ears and the neck. I had never ever seen Pat's neck or her ears for that matter. The image of Pat walking into class that day has stayed with me for fifty one years.

Transformed, the swan, *Cinderella*, and *Sleeping Beauty*, Pat's transformation was stunning. She was beautiful, unique, glassless, a real beauty. Pat had turquoise eyes enhanced by her new blue contact lenses. She was gorgeous. If only Vidal Sasson knew how his five point haircut had changed the image of Pat. An image so powerful, it remains sacred in my memory to share with strangers who might listen to my story, a memory found not lost.

It happened in High School an "image-changing" event, a stunning transformation, to savor, and to pay homage. A simple little haircut had the power to effect such change and leave a lasting impression on me all these years.

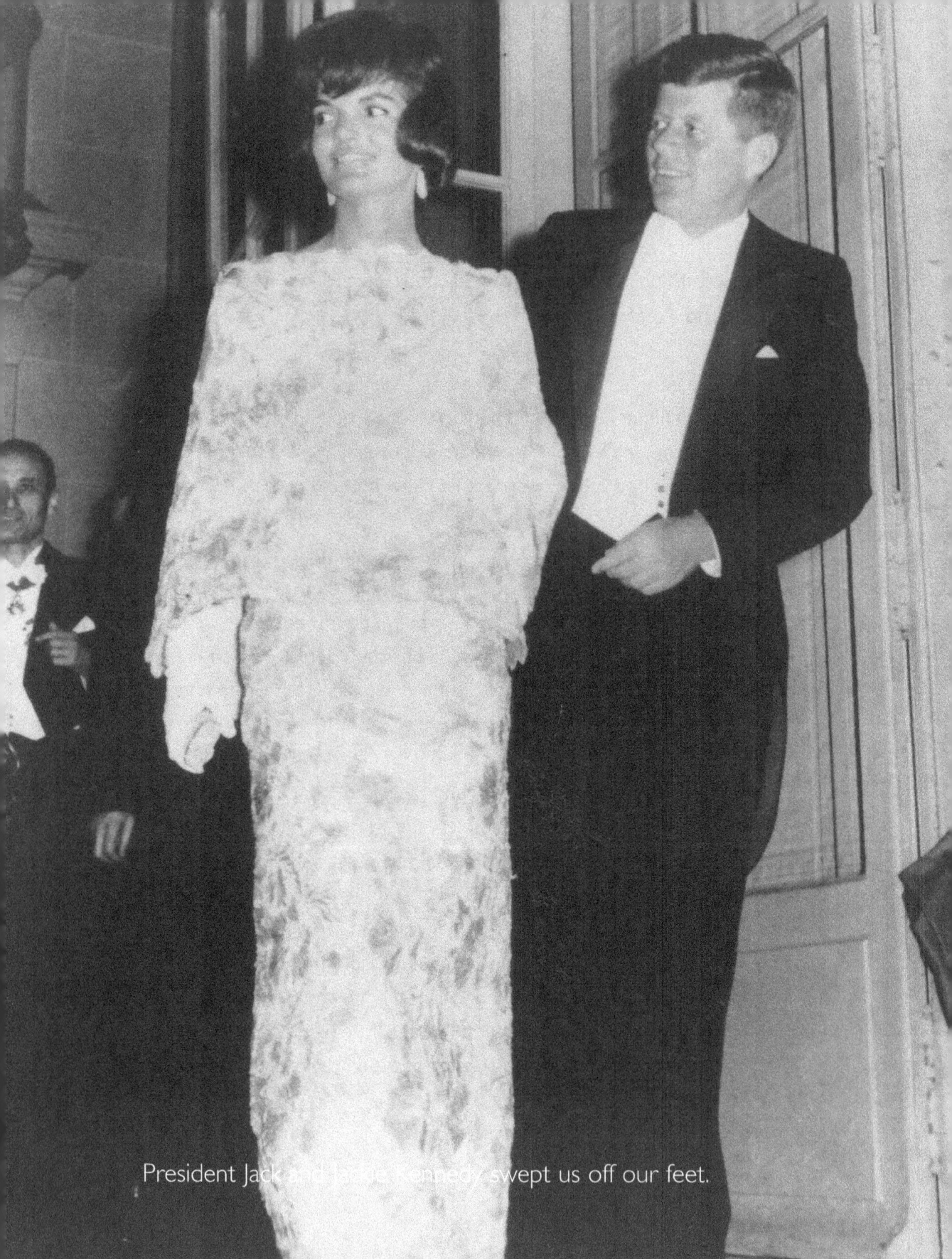

President Jack and Jackie Kennedy swept us off our feet.

CHAPTER 5
JACK AND JACKIE

"There's a man with a gun over there
Telling me I got to beware
It's time we stop,
Hey what's that sound?
Everybody look what's going down."

Buffalo Springfield

Knowing the past is helpful in understanding the present, how we got to where we are and the people who helped get us there.

Florence, Italy in the renaissance period was a center burgeoning with art, sculpture, and painting: Leonardo Di Vinci, Michelangelo, and Raphael. Paris in the 1870s was the hub of Rodin's sculptures and the impressionistic period in painting, Claude Monet, Eduardo Manet, Renoir, Van Gogh, and Seurat. It was a concentration of creative energy in one area proliferating outward. The father of Jungian psychology Jung called it collective consciousness; an archetypical energy radiating from the unconscious and extending out ward to the external world.

London in the sixties was like Florence and Paris, a mecca brimming with creativity. The music groups included were called: The Beatles, The Dave Clark Five, The Animals, Herman and the Hermits, The Rolling Stones, and the Who. In the fashion world Mary Quant knocked us all out with her mini skirt. The new fashion models of the moment were Jean Shrimpton and Twiggy both the new celebrities to emulate and adore.

London's hair stylist Vidal Sassoon added his genius with the look of small precision haircuts to wear with our new mini skits sans Peggy Moffat. The five point haircut was born and a new look was launched. We were the young models of the new modern..... We were "MOD". The style was so innovative it exploded across the Atlantic. We were united by an international force not to be equaled for many generations to come.

The mood of the Sixties was favoring the youth of the culture, and it reached many spheres of our life. The media labeled it the "youth quake" and it indeed shook the world.

Youth filtered into the politics of a nation. We were switching from leaders who looked older. The politicians of the current genre all looked like our grandfathers. The presidents Harry Truman and General Eisenhower and their wives Bess and Mamie were much older and more conservative in their fashion and their hair didn't have the style or the verve that soon would be coming. A much younger man in his early forties was seeking the office of the presidency and with his wife they would sweep us off our feet.

John Fitzgerald Kennedy and his beautiful wife, Jacqueline, would set the standard for a new look in the political structure. We became Jack and Jackie watchers. Everything they did or said interested us, we couldn't get enough. From the moment of the inauguration in January, of 1961, Jackie Kennedy and her fashion reigned. Oleg Cassini designed her outfit for the event. Mrs. Kennedy wore a hat at the crown of her head and it was coined the pillbox. Hats were not worn much before this time but now the millinery factories were back in business. The Jackie hat would be worn in different fabrics and colors and we fell in love with the look. From the moment she stood next to him on the inaugural platform on that cold and windy day in Washington, the style she created was an image seared in our style brain and we had to have it.

Jackie was the style icon of clothes, jewelry and hair. Mr. Kenneth was her hair dresser and he was at the Elizabeth Arden Salon in New York. Kenneth designed and created her now famous bouffant hair style. If she changed her part it was news worthy. If she let her hair grow, we let our hair grow. You could not attend a wedding, bar mitzvah, church or temple without seeing Jackie Kennedy "look-a-likes." They were everywhere. Going to work and looking out the window of the bus stood a "Jackie" on every corner. It spread like a virus.

When the Kennedys traveled abroad to different countries; crowds by the thousands gathered to get a glimpse of our Rock stars. The fans were screaming in the streets of Paris, Berlin, Ireland and Mexico. They were our uncrowned King and Queen and we were finally "royal." There was a widely acclaimed show on Broadway at this time called *Camelot* that represented a mythical and magical kingdom where might works at the service of right and as a symbol of collaboration and unity. The Kennedy years in the White House were compared to this utopian vision of *Camelot*.

A decade that started with such splendor ended with such horror. On November 22, 1963 several bullets discharged from high powered guns brought a country to its knees. President Kennedy was dead as was his kingdom of *Camelot*. Where we were at the moment of the assassination was our personal history we would remember and always share. We were closer as a generation sharing our shock and grief together; we just were not ready to bury our hero so young.

On April 4th, 1968 another American hero Martin Luther King was shot down in his prime fighting for a better life for others. We were sickened at another brilliant leader shot down and taken away from us by an assassin's bullet. How could this happen?

Robert Kennedy, the once and future king we hoped would rekindle *Camelot*... murdered on June 5th, 1968. How could this happen? Fifty years later, we're still asking the same question.

New images emerged from these tragedies. The widows of each of these slain men Jaqueline Kennedy, Coretta King, Ethel Kennedy all carried themselves with beauty and dignity and they were an example for us to follow. I often wonder if anyone of them realized how they helped a country to heal. If they could get through these horrific events we could. The powerful images of these three widows at different times in the sixties were a display of grace that helped a nation to come to terms with these events.

The assassination of John Fitzgerald Kennedy clearly changed everything for this generation. We were all murdered the day the President of the United States was shot right before our eyes; the illusion of safety in our country was shattered along with our innocence. The flavor of the sixties was an amalgam of many significant events. It was the beginning or foreshadowing of shocking events that would follow.

CHAPTER 6
THE WEDDING ALBUM

"Scattered pictures
Of the smiles we left behind
Smiles we gave to one another
For the way we were."

Music by Marvin Hamlisch, Lyrics by Alan and Marilyn Bergman

I like to spend quiet moments alone in the early morning hours relaxing in a comfortable arm chair, with a familiar cup of coffee. I especially like to linger over old photo albums or scrapbooks. I particularly like to look at my wedding album from 1967. I do this more often then I'd like to admit because I like the way I look in those pictures. Anyone who knows me well would be surprised to learn this fact because I hate taking pictures, and even worse looking at myself in them. It is distressing and even painful for me. But I like the way I look in the photographs of myself in 1967 at my wedding in Chicago at the Belden Stratford Hotel.

The weddings of today are much more extravagant and cost tons more money. No matter what the expense of the wedding they all share the incredible joy and fun of friends and families coming together in celebration of finding love and getting married.

Looking at the photographs in my wedding album, I marvel at the young bride who is staring back at me; her face without wrinkles, a face that gravity and age haven't diminished yet. There is no evidence of her future children,

Robert, Jonathan, and Laura. Certainly there is no sign of their future children Katie, Jason, Allison and Ruthie. Her future is all ahead of her. How clear eyed and sure she appears in the photograph without any clue of the mistakes she will make and the lessons she will learn. How quickly life will take her hand and shake her clarity and end her innocence. Looking in a mirror can never reflect who you were; only a photograph can do that.

I also appreciate having the album so I can see dear friends and relatives who are no longer present in our lives. This gives me an opportunity to reflect on their stories and what their contributions were to my life. Everyone you know has a story to tell, lately, but I just can't find anyone who will listen to mine; maybe Ruthie, my granddaughter, will.

My mother and Aunt Katie struggled for days with the seating plans for the wedding. The problem with the seating was there was always a relative fighting with another family member and they wouldn't speak to one another for years. Or someone didn't invite someone to a party and someone from the party said something about someone that they weren't supposed to tell anyone; and now the one who told is angry at the one who told the one who wasn't even at the party. This reminds me of the famous comedy routine from the Abbott and Costello 1938 radio show, *Who's on first?*

After college I moved to New York from Chicago in the latter sixties. Four girlfriends and I lived in a one bedroom apartment on 69th between park and Lexington. I met the man I was to marry in New York after a three month courtship. My wedding dress was bought at Macys at the cost of one hundred dollars. I loved the dress; it had appliqued daisies all over it. Daisies were my favorite flower, so I knew it was meant to be.

The wedding dress I wore was great, but my hair said everything. I had cut my shoulder length hair short when I moved from Chicago to celebrate my new freedom in New York City. Vidal Sassoon would take it to a new level of chic a week before the wedding. That haircut I would wear for the next forty six years of my life. It would range in various incarnations of color to the present white.

Vidal Sassoon, genius extraordinaire, raised the bar on an industry just waiting for him. He saw hair from a geometric perspective as an architect would. It would become the foundation for all precision haircuts of the future. His look was the epitome of fashion that led the way internationally and in the United States. No one since has contributed more to hairstyling. His work still reverberates through time and is still relevant. He made hair an art form and his schools still carry on the legend. Handsome, classy, charming and brilliant; thank God we have the pictures of his work to celebrate his innovative artistry.

A small hat covered with the same appliqued daisies as the dress was worn at the crown of my head, 'ala' Jackie Kennedy. The veil was attached to the hat and descended down my back and then puddled to the floor. It was perfect. How lucky I was to be able to be living in New York and go to the Vidal Sassoon's salon on Madison Avenue where he himself cut my hair. It was quite daring for a bride to have such a short haircut, but I always liked looking different and not like everyone else. I felt incredibly beautiful the day of my wedding and I thank Vidal Sassoon for that. Never underestimate the power of a haircut.

I hope professional hair stylists realize the responsibility they have for doing a client's hair and makeup for their special events. The images created will be permanent. The photographs become more precious with time and increase in value because the moment can never be duplicated or recaptured again.

The bride, years later when overwhelmed by life and laundry can renew herself by looking at her image in the photo album and recalling how she looked in her enchanted moment. Time frozen and images preserved, she will be grateful to have the album for reflection and regeneration of her spirit as a remembrance of her once upon a time fairy tale wedding.

Hair professionals have the opportunity and the obligation to give their best on those occasions because the images reflected on film are the visual rendering of their client's story, to treasure and give pleasure for years to come.

One morning the bride many years older, will be sitting quietly alone in a comfortable arm chair with a familiar cup of coffee lingering over the pictures from her wedding album and lovingly remembering "the way they all were."

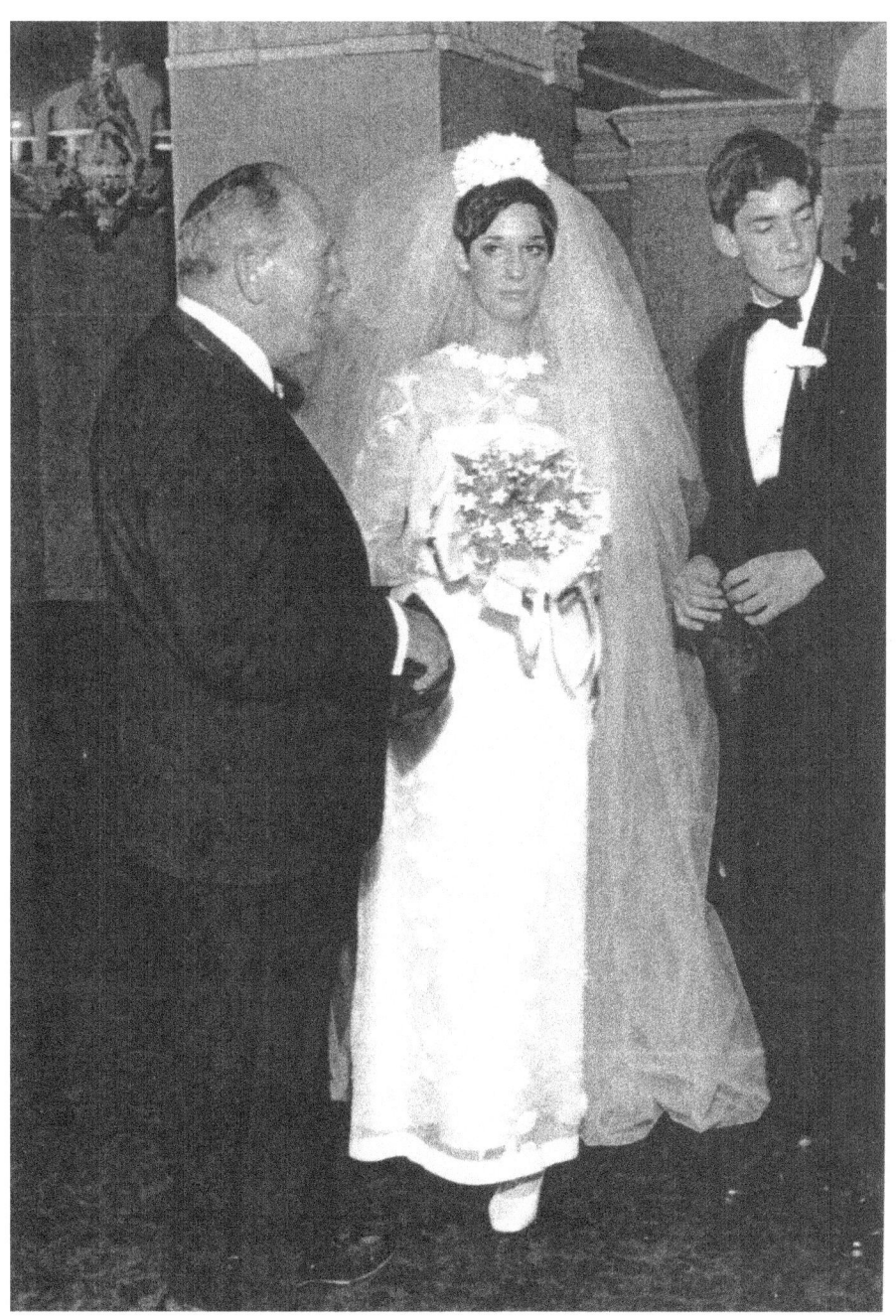

Never underestimate the power of a haircut.

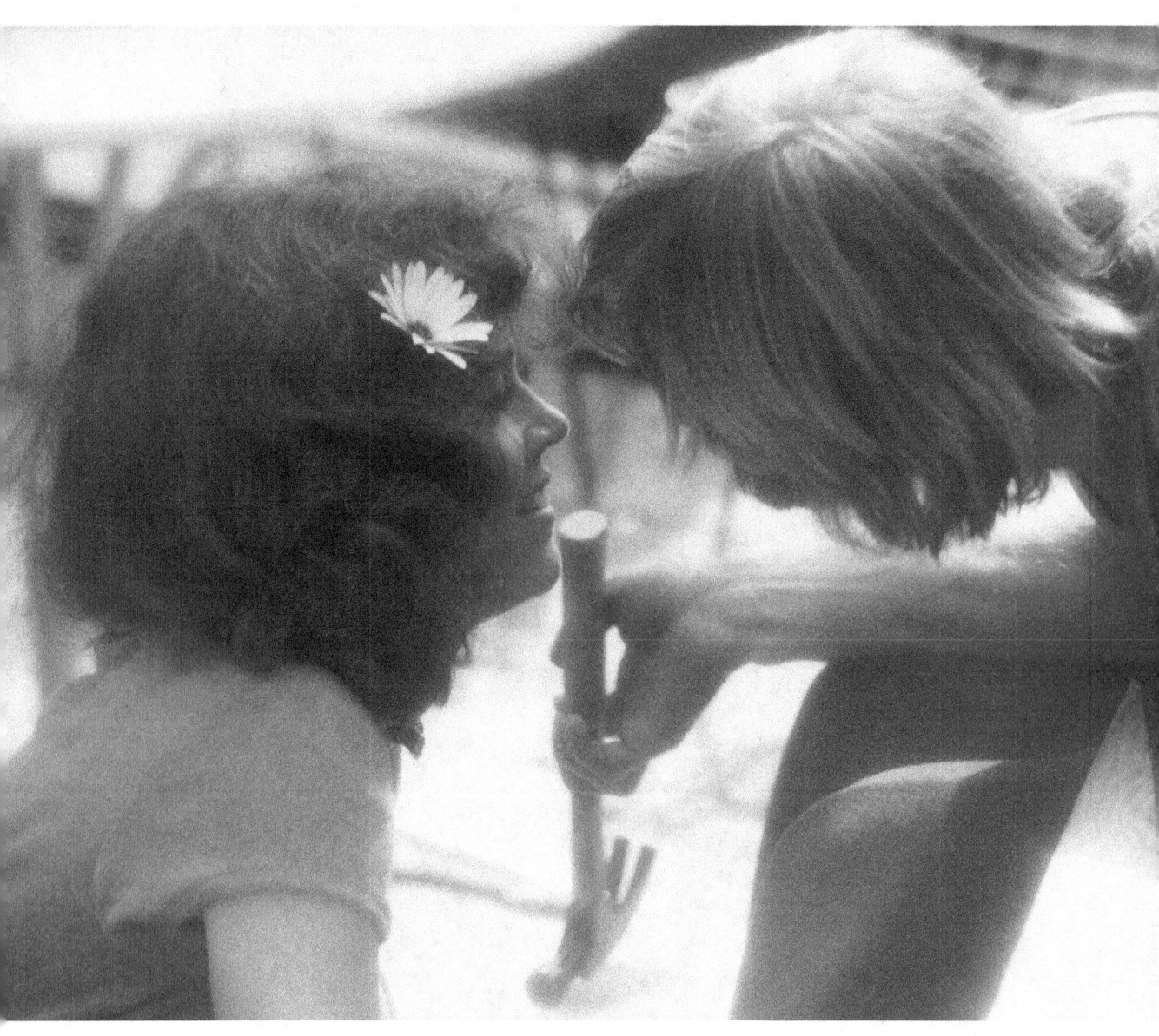

Jane Fonda and Jon Voight in the movie, *Coming Home*.

CHAPTER 7
THE SEVENTIES
AND HAIR AS PROTEST

"Where have all the flowers gone?
Long time passing
Where have all the flowers gone?
Long time ago"

Pete Seeger: *Where have all the Flowers Gone*

The 'Seventies' music was much more thoughtful and profound then the previous decade. The lyrics were protests against the establishment and mistrust of anyone over forty. Mistrust of the military sending our young men into the war in Vietnam. In those years the military had the Draft and thousands of young men were sent to fight in Viet Nam and they didn't know the truthful reasons why they were asked to kill and possibly give up their lives. The television's nightly news listed the dead soldiers' names across the screens at the end of every telecast. Each night hundreds of names appeared; mother and father's sons, husbands of wives, fathers of children, sisters losing brothers, neighbor's sons, and best friends losing each another. Everyone in our country knew someone who went to war and was badly wounded or killed in Vietnam.

We lost faith in our government and didn't believe anything that our leaders had to say. We wanted to know the truth; and we knew the killings had to stop. We protested in the streets, we had sit-ins and marches on college campuses.

On May 4th, 1970 four Kent State students were murdered on the campus of Kent State. They were shot by the Ohio National Guard: William Schuler, Allison Krause, Jeffery Miller, and Sandra Scheur. It was a day of infamy and shame for the United States. Young and innocent unarmed students were shot and killed protesting on a college campus because they wanted the war to end and they wanted the truth from their leaders.

Crosby, Stills, Nash and Young sang a song in political protest, *The Soldiers and Nixon Were Coming.* They were demonstrating the brutality at Kent State. When they performed, their hair was styled long with bandanas wrapped around their forehead, Cherokee Indian style. Their hair was a symbolic reminder to the country and projected the ideals they thought we were losing; hair became a metaphor for protest and change.

There was an extraordinary movie in 1978 called *Coming Home.* Jane Fonda and John Voight were the principal characters in the movie. John Voight won the Academy Award as best actor for the role he played that year. He portrayed a Vietnam veteran who came home crippled and handicapped by the war and was confined to a wheelchair. His character was disillusioned by the war and with the establishment; in protest he wore his hair very long. Jon Voight played Luke Martin in the film and his hair became the metaphor for his angst and anti-establishment viewpoint. This was in direct contrast to Bruce Dern who played a Marine officer in the war and he wore his hair much shorter, both characters hair symbolizing each ones political perspectives and protest against the war.

Jane Fonda's hair also had a dramatic transition. Her internal evolution of consciousness was symbolized by the freeing of her hair in the movie. Early in the movie she had a very controlled hair style, which transitioned into a rebellious and unmanaged hairstyle of waves and curls. All three of these actors used hair as a metaphor for their beliefs about the war in Vietnam. Without saying a word their hair spoke metaphorically about their values and how they felt.

The seventies were an important time for change in our country. Most people hate change and if you brought it, they reacted negatively to you. It wasn't easy. Everyone from the older generation hated the long hair and battles ensued over a couple of inches. Fathers would not speak to their sons for not getting their hair cut. The disgust and anger about the length of hair was palpable. Without these brave young heroines and heroes going up against the older generation we wouldn't have ended the Vietnam War in 1976 or started the strong activism of the women's movement fighting against discrimination in this country.

Another icon of the seventies was African-American Angela Davis. She was a political activist rallying for social change, combatting oppression racially and economically. Black is beautiful and she was the perfect symbol of just that. Angela Davis wore her hair in a big, beautiful Afro which said let our hair be natural and authentic. Angela Davis' hair and look was as powerful as her words. Her hair style caught the imagination of everyone; men and women of every race adopted the look and were inspired to wear their hair like hers.

We can't leave this decade without the mention of the iconic Gloria Steinem. The face of feminism—and what a face! She was one of the founding leaders and a spokesperson for women's issues, writer, organizer, journalist, and editor and founder of *MS magazine*; she was a vital feminist and gifted inspiration to the women's movement. We owe so much to her brilliance in making the world better for women. We stood breathless as we listened and watched her speaking for us. Standing with her long beautiful hair, and her aviator glasses, she was tall and resplendent in her mini-skirt as she spoke to the crowds brilliantly. Gloria Steinem was our spokesperson and her image was a sustaining force not to be reckoned with. How proud she made us.

The enduring visual images of these iconic political activists served as a metaphor for change in this country. Their fighting spirit provoked and motivated us to change our world.

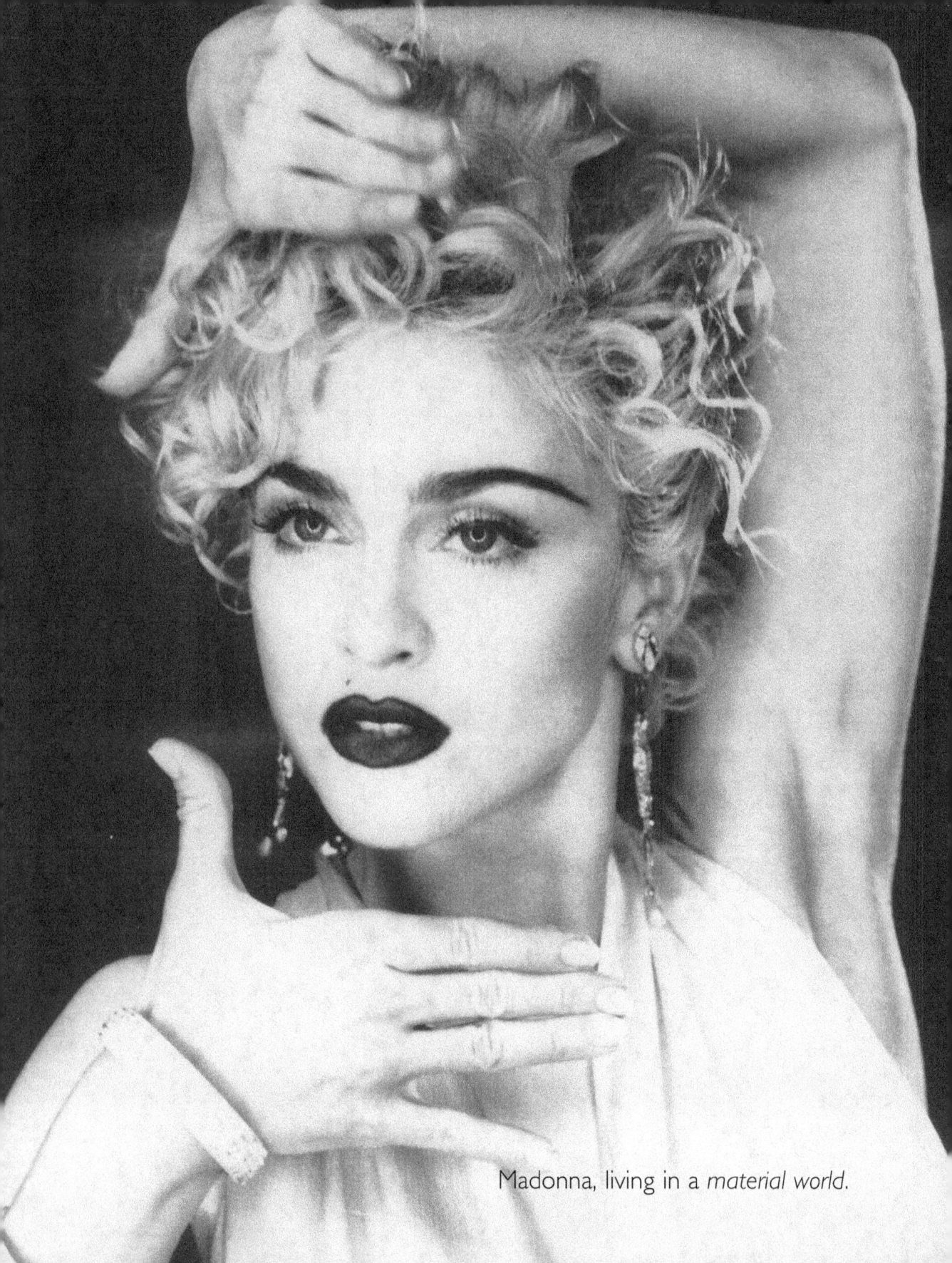

Madonna, living in a *material world*.

CHAPTER 8
THE EIGHTIES AND NINTIES AND MATERIAL GIRLS

"Living in a material world
And I am a material girl
You know we are living in a material world
            and I am a material girl."

Lyrics to *A Material Girl* by Madonna

The sixties and seventies were serious and productive decades. Enormous legislation was passed in this country trying to make life better for the majority. Protests, marches on Washington and on college campuses brought about the changes needed to save people's lives and end injustices. Never has a generation been more conscious of their fellow countrymen and the desire to change things. They were fighting government systems and big business, a generation of men and women to whom we owe a great debt.

July 2, 1964 The Civil Rights Amendment was passed.

In 1976 the Viet Nam war ended.

Single handedly Rachel Carson author of *Silent Spring* fought the corporation Monsanto on the effects of pesticides on our air and water. The book documented the detrimental effects of chemicals on the environment urging President Johnson to pass a law called the *Clean Air Act* in 1970. We were all entitled to have water and our air free of pollutants.

Betty Friedan established the National Organization for Women, fighting for the rights of women and successfully making birth control for women legal in 1967.

Two reporters for the Washington Post Bob Woodward and Carl Bernstein exposed Watergate to the public bringing down a sitting President forcing the resignation of President Nixon on August 8, 1974.

Remarkable men like Caesar Chavez took up the fight for the rights of migrant workers.

There will never be another generation of men and women who cared and did more to create change in this country.

Were we ready for what was ahead for us? Were we ready for new fashions the new hair styles and the music the children of the eighties and nineties decades would bring? They would startle the world with a technology revolution and achieve commercial and media advancements through the Internet and the World Wide Web. Under the guise of Globalization, the manufacturing base of America moved to China, Thailand, Mexico South Korea, and Taiwan. Multinational corporations, rapid economic growth and the personal computer took over. The groundwork was laid for Pac Man, Nintendo, Game Boy and Mario. David Scrota's book *The Other Eighties* exclaimed about "Rubic's Cube" and "Where's the Beef?"

The anger and protesting from the sixties and seventies was being replaced by a cockiness and confidence unlike their predecessors. Entitlement was a new word added to our vocabulary. Were we ready for the song that would represent the eighties and Cyndi Lauper was going to sing to us in 1983 that "Girls just want to have fun."

My father yells what you gonna do with your life
Oh daddy dear you know you're still number one

Oh girls just want to have fun
That's all they really want—some fun.

The trend of the eighties was big shoulder pads and leggings. Hair, like Cyndi Lauper's song was also about fun. Big, bigger and biggest was the style and we would get there with perms and lots of aerosol cans of Rayette. We were of the idea that bigger was better, and more was not enough. Madonna's left her roots dark and mixed it up with her blond hair and the look was enviable. Ponytails usually worn at the center back of the head were now featured on the side, looking cool when worn with their denim and lace.

John Hughes made a series of movies focusing on high school life and teenage angst; starring Molly Ringwald in *Sixteen Candles*, 1984; *Breakfast Club*, 1985; *Ferris Bueller* and *Pretty in Pink*, 1986. His *Home Alone* movies were all hits, one two, and three. Looking at the lives of these high schoolers opened up a new market to yield new earnings. High school was the fresh target and profit center for big business and the movie industry.

The Brat Pack had their own individual style and hair; there were no rules, choice was whatever they wanted it to be. Molly Ringwald, Ally Sheedy, Rob Lowe, Judd Nelson, and Andrew McCarthy were the new emerging teen idols. It just wasn't a buffet of hair choices we had a veritable hair smorgasbord to choose from.

Fare thee well "hippies" and "yippies," Madonna was now going to sing about the *Material Girl* and was opening the doorway way for the decade's conspicuous consumption. The television shows were about the families of rich and the super-rich. We were all their slaves until the next weekly episode aired. Joan Collins was the beautiful and dangerous Alexis in *Dynasty,* with

Linda Evans as Krystle the good, both vying for the attention of the powerful Blake Carrington. Alexis and Krystle both wore large shoulder pads in their designer dresses and their hair extended beyond their shoulders; both fighting up to the very last installment of the show. Sue Ellen in the show *Dallas* was always up against Victoria Principle. The nation was biting their fingernails until we found out who shot J.R. Ewing. The Colbys and *Knots Landing*, *Falcon Crest* were also getting our attention weekly.

We were on a roller coaster of fun and Indiana Jones was going to take us on the ride of our life. If you wanted a different type of excitement, who you gonna call? *Ghostbusters*. For an even more out of this world experience, we would watch *E. T.* and fall in love with this lovable alien.

The last part of the eighties brought an iconic image of hair that endeared children and adults alike. It was Ariel of the beauteous red hair in *The Little Mermaid*. The animation gave us a stunning representation of Ariel's hair moving deliciously underwater and it was one of the best looks of the decade in 1989. Ariel's dazzling red hair color influenced our own hair color and opened us to a wider spectrum of reds including the pinks and purples we wear today. These choices opened new dimensions of color that were never seen before or worn on our grand strands. Hair lovers and hair dreamers now made *A Rainbow Connection.*

Ahead for us would be the new images of super women as in the television show *Charley's Angels* with the iconic hair styles of Farrah Fawcett, Kate Jackson, and Jaclyn Smith. Their shiny tresses dazzled us as did their beauty, brains, brawn and volume. We would all try to emulate Farrah's wondrous hair and copy her iconic look. Once again another hair style went viral and was seen on everyone, everywhere. We finally had ultimate hair freedom.

The first cell phone sold was on March 13, 1984, for $ 3,995.00. We were

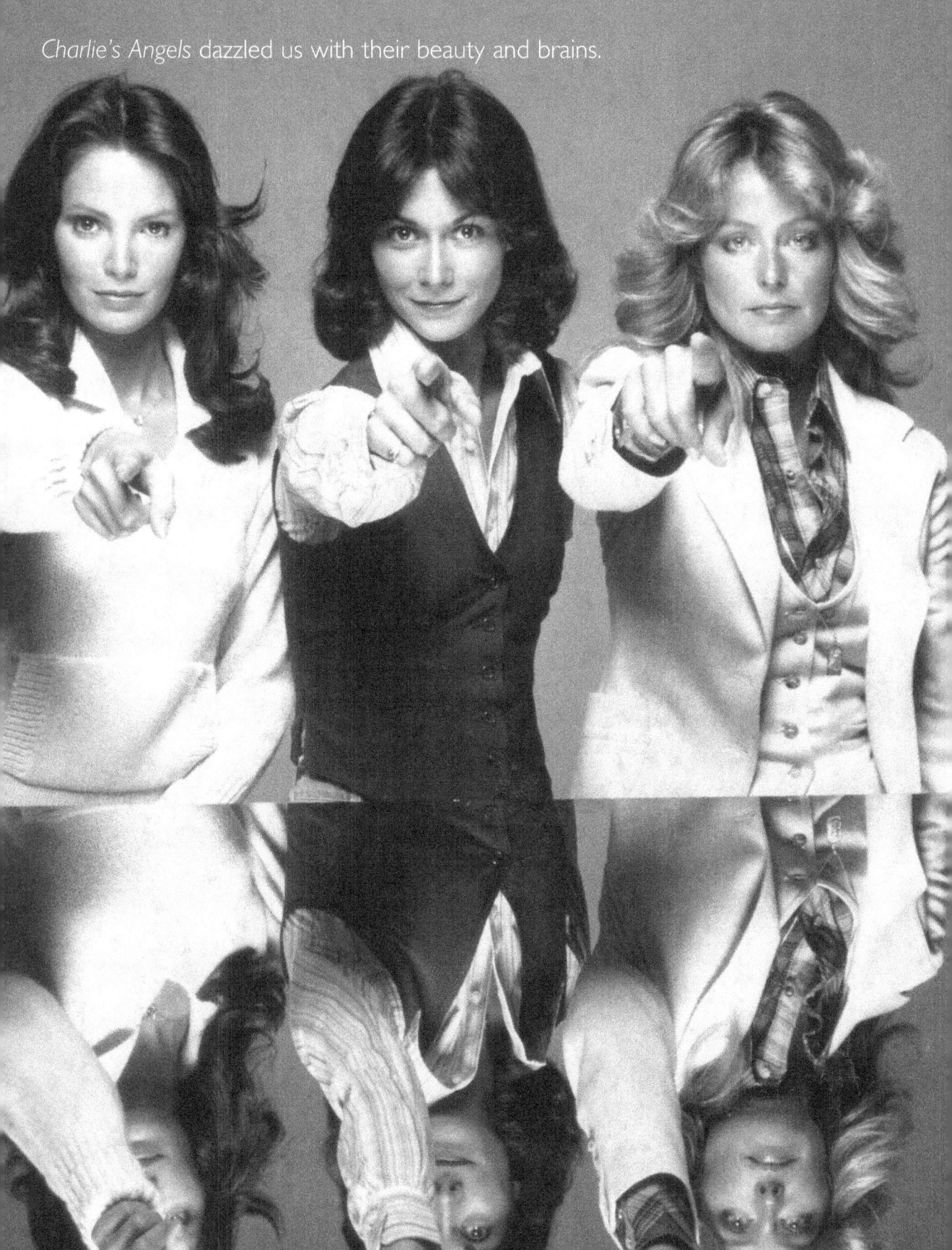

Charlie's Angels dazzled us with their beauty and brains.

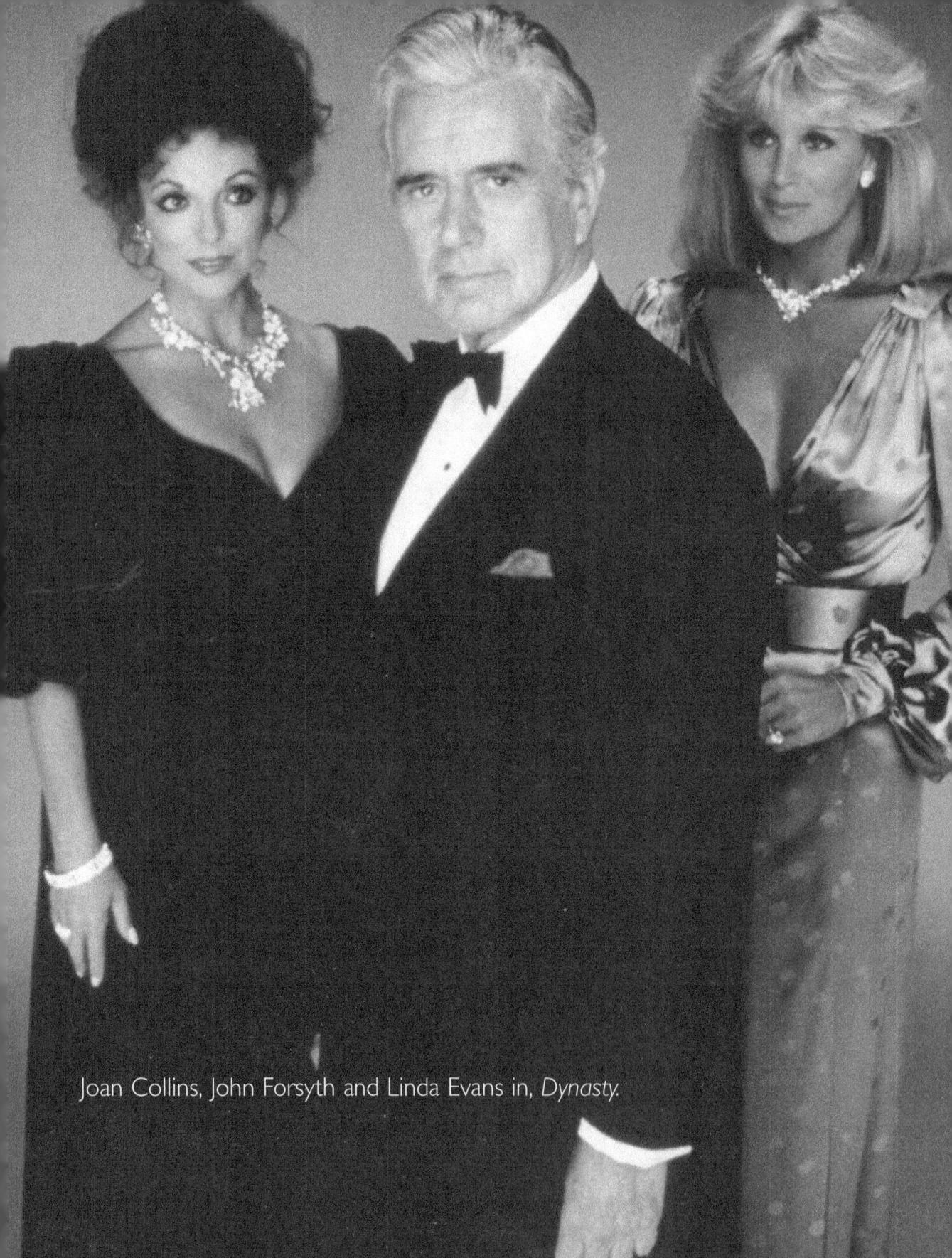

Joan Collins, John Forsyth and Linda Evans in, *Dynasty*.

now going to be able to talk to each other anywhere any time of the day or night. The crime fighting detective of the 1940's comic strip, *Dick Tracy* boggled our minds with the phone wristwatch he wore to communicate his crime fighting tactics. That wrist phone seemed so far off into the future but the farfetched idea arrived and was here. We didn't have the wristband to wear like *Dick Tracy*, but cell phones would be in our pockets and purses and like the credit cards we would never leave home without them.

The funsters of this generation were the beginning of the millennium generation and they were all having so much fun with the new technology. In the next decades the games would become more sophisticated and evolve into the world-changing Facebook and texting. Ahead the selfie would evolve and having great hair would be a requisite for the images of this millennium generation.

I don't text much and I miss conversation with my coworkers at lunch. They are always busy texting and Facebooking. Fun for me is not technology but arguing politics and if the current war is ethical or not. Sixties people cut their teeth on debating at the dining room table. Today it is not politically correct to ask if you're a Democrat or Republican. I'm really not having very much fun. I miss the seventies.

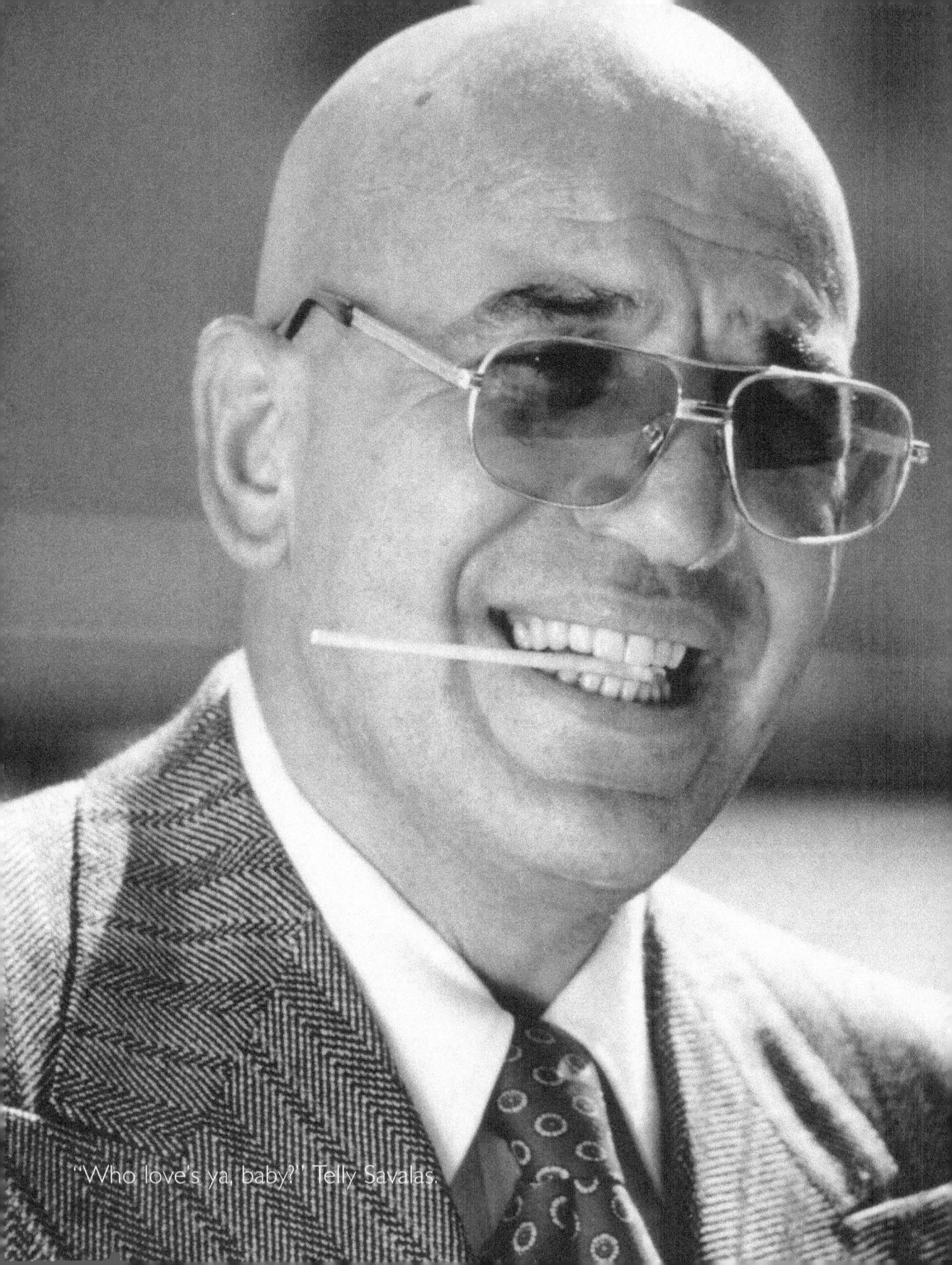
"Who love's ya, baby?" Telly Savalas.

CHAPTER 9
THE MILLINEUM AND BALD IS BEAUTIFUL

"I'm too sexy for my love
To sexy for my love
I'm too sexy for this song"

By Fred and Richard Fairbrass, Rob Manzoli

Some may argue when the millennium began. Some researchers and commentators say it was 1980 to the early 2000. In spite of the questionable time line as to when it occurred, a remarkable new trend started and changed the way people thought, and a new conversation began. At this time a different image was created which brought a new visual to the world stage and changed an old concept for so many. A new set of standards that never existed before, or may have not been as prevalent, brought the idea forth and it exploded and became a new path for us to follow and admire.

The trend ignited new criteria for the male of our species. The splendidly naked head on the human male was now considered to be beautiful and enormously sexy. This was a vastly different attitude then in decades past when baldness was considered to be a characteristic of a mature man or a man who appeared to look much older compared to the younger and hairier counterparts. Men who felt loss or shame by having less hair were now suddenly able to feel more masculine and powerful.

Never before did men like Ben Kingsley who was personified as the *Sexy*

Beast, or likewise Bruce Willis in his *Die Hard* Movies became sex symbols as did with the very cool Michael Jordan. When did bald become beautiful and the ultimate masculine and charismatic sex symbol as seen on the newest sexy rapper Pitbull. When did this happen? Shaving their heads fully of any hair contributed to the myth making status.

I remember my sweet Uncle Lester of my childhood, who always had a cigarette dangling from his lips and a pack of Chesterfields in the pocket of his white short sleeve shirt. He was the only uncle who would sit with us at the kids table on the holidays and seemed truly interested in talking to us and listening to what we had to say. He was a wonderful man but he was bald very, very early. To me, he never seemed cool or sexy, just the lovely Uncle of my youth. Hymie also from the same holiday table (but the grown up one) loved the brisket almost as much as the six strands of shiny hair he carefully oiled and glued individually and placed across the empty space on the top of his head.

Comb overs were a man's way of still maintaining a youthful look. Hair was parted and grew heavily on one side of the head and would then be carefully combed over to connect to the other side of the wearers head. Hair products and sprays or hidden hair pins would then try to secure the creative hair bridge. But the consequences could be disastrous on a windy day. I have been witness to a comb over lift two feet above the wearers head in one large piece. Toupees and comb overs were some of the tools available as camouflage for the ubiquitous hairless. Probably the most famous comb over is Donald Trumps and I don't know anyone who doesn't want to comb, shave or change it.

When did baldness, for lack of a better word, become the sex symbol it is now? I am trying to put together a reasonable history of sexy men who shaved their heads completely before the new millennium. One remarkably stunning man stands out among the many.

That man was the indomitable Yul Brynner. For those who have not experienced that captivating Russian you missed something. He starred in the role of a lifetime as the King of Siam in the Rogers and Hammerstein's stage play *The King and I* in 1951. It was also made into a motion picture film of in 1956 as well. I believe it was a first for audiences to glimpse his perfectly proportioned head shaved in all its beauty. His masculinity was magnetic whenever he appeared in any of his movies, *The Brothers Karamazov*, *Anastasia,* and *The Magnificent Seven.* Elegant in black turtle neck sweaters a fierce image not to be missed. Try to see some of his movies. It's definitely worth your time.

Moving to the seventies 1973 to 1978, another Bald Beauty thrilled and mesmerized our night time television evenings. This was Telly Savalas as New York Detective Lieutenant Theo in the series of *Kojak*. He alone was able to get my father to give up listening to a sporting event on the radio to watch the Kojak series with the family. Not many things could get my father off the couch in the living room when he was listening to the excited rantings of his favorite sports announcer Jack Brickhouse, from his beloved burgundy colored Zenith radio.

Everybody loved *Kojak*. His famous line from the show that we waited anxiously to hear him say weekly was "Who loves ya baby?" Those words were amplified by the trademark lollipop he carried and enjoyed. Well, we loved Ya Telly, and the legions of men and women watching his show were all captivated and charmed by his naked head, season after season.

These men were the ground breakers for the "Pitbulls" and all the sexy men who followed. Fearless and confident men that made the transformation possible when years before they were the butt of jokes, they now commandeered an image that was as popular as the rock stars of the day who were flaunting their overgrown locks. Icons like Aero Smiths, Steven Tyler, Rolling stones, Keith Richards, Led Zeppelin, Jon Bon Jovi and Richie Sambora, or Joe Elliot of Def Leppard. I'm still waiting and hoping for Ian Fleming's sexy 007 to join in this conversation and shed and shave his noble strands.

If nature and DNA designed less hair for an individual, some took what they were given and made lemonade, while others hid under a toupee. I applaud the ground breakers that don't cover their baldness and inspire and give confidence to people and provide new standards of value for the self. People in the media have a platform and if their influence is used well, they can serve their fellow inhabitants of this planet by promoting healthy and authentic images men can follow.

Women today are using the same concept of a naked head or less hair as also being beautiful and sexy without the stigma of shame or heartbreak attached to it. Women and men are not letting the loss of their hair define who they are and how they feel about themselves. Beauty as a standard requires different points of view especially where less can be more. A smaller silhouette can enhance features on a face that were never really revealed before and produce a dramatic and exciting new look and result. After all, it's all about the base…. bout the base…. bout the base.

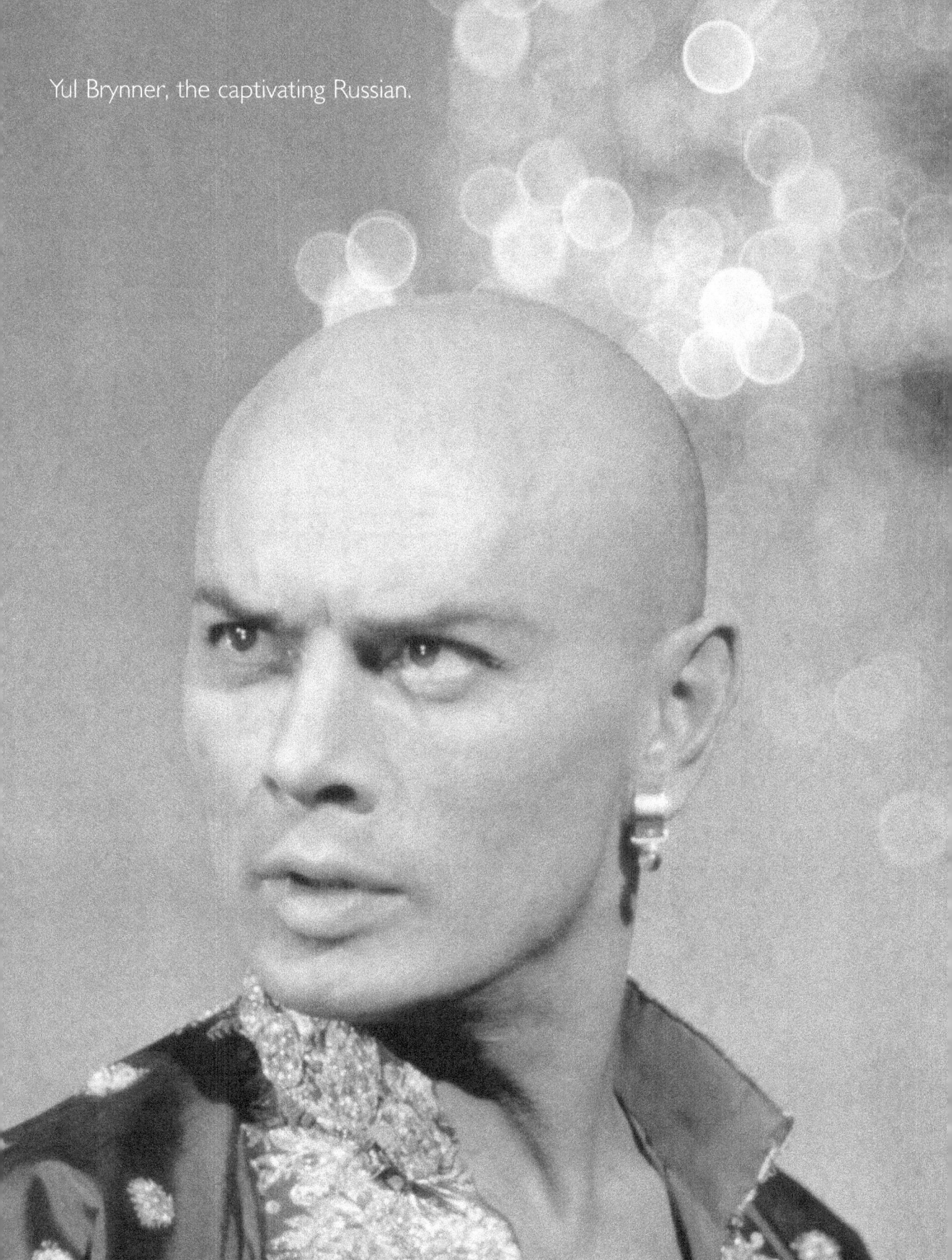

Yul Brynner, the captivating Russian.

Cary Grant and Grace Kelly, a pairing of unparalleled good taste..

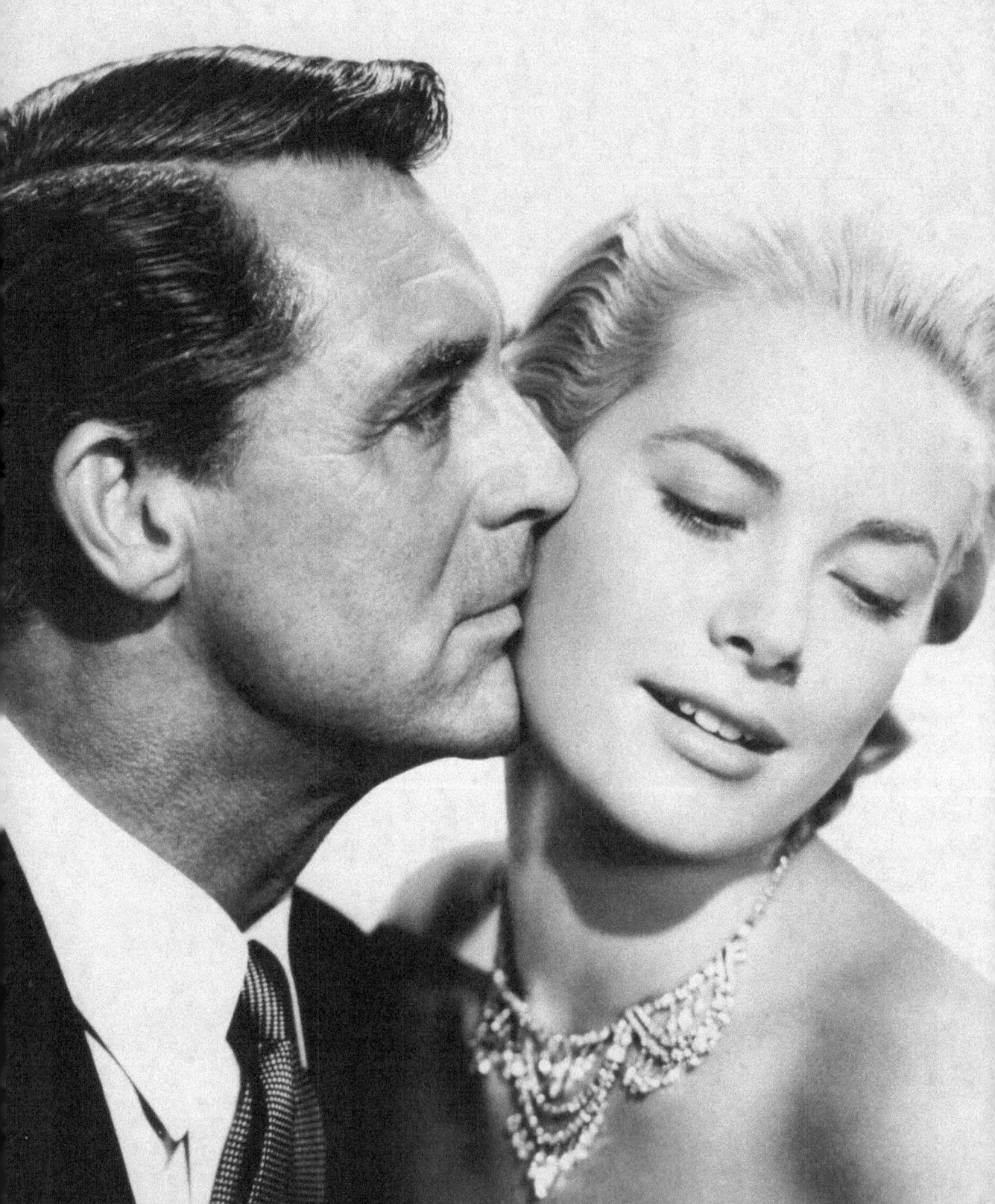

CHAPTER 10
HAIR A CELEBRITIES TRADEMARK
(to admire, love and follow)

"Moon River
Wider than a mile;
I'm crossing you in style someday"

Johnny Mercer and Henry Mancini in the movie *Moon River*

Hair is a trademark of the celebrity. A hairs color, cut, and style is enormously important in the creation and selection of the projected image a celebrity wants to be known for. Careful thought and guidance from experts all contribute to a successful look for the celebrity and for all of us to admire, love and follow.

Can you imagine Marilyn Monroe, not as a blond or Jean Harlow not the blond bombshell of the Thirties? They certainly were not born that blond. It was a stroke of genius to pile the bleach on their hair to make them look blonder. The flash of platinum created a look and a standard for all sexy blonds to come. The phrase "dumb blondes" could not apply to those two women.

Veronica Lake the queen of the forties film noir movies wore her hair in long waves just past her shoulder and parted to one side that hung over covering one eye. The nation adopted the look which was the forerunner to

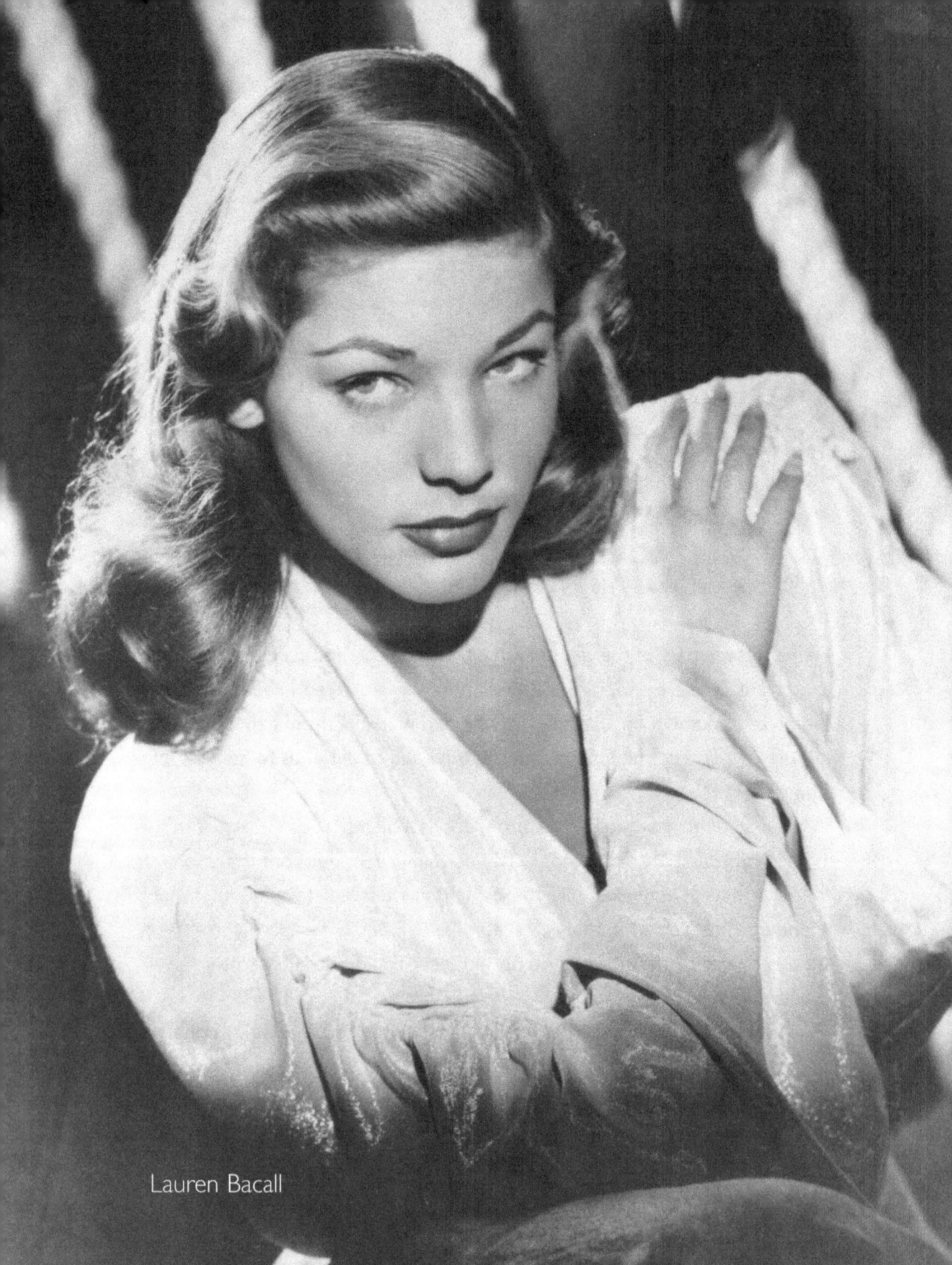
Lauren Bacall

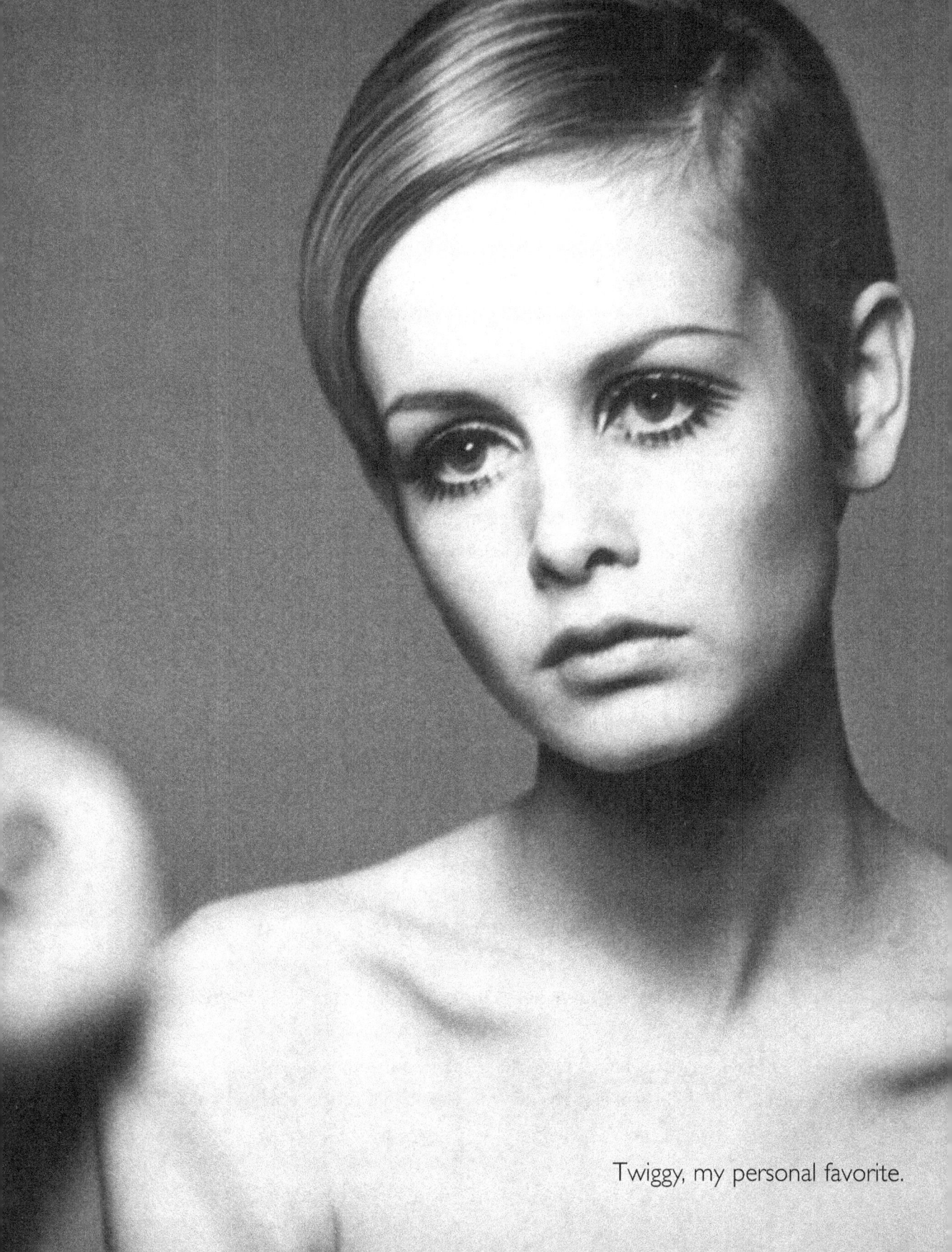

Twiggy, my personal favorite.

Jessica Rabbit of Toon Town from the movie, *Who Killed Roger Rabbit* in 1988.

Lauran Bacall's sexy long "page boy" was featured in the movie, *To Have and Have Not.* The star Humphrey Bogart fell hard for that pageboy and had to have her and marry her, in the movie as well as in real life. Ingrid Bergman's Hemingway's story, *For Whom the Bell Tolls* was never more beautiful with her short cropped hair glistening in the Spanish Mountains. Gary Cooper couldn't resist running his hands through her Ingrid's hair and he fell madly in love in the movie. Who wouldn't want Gary Cooper's fingers running through their hair? The beautiful women we never got tired of looking at. Decades later their images are still legendary by their style, beauty and trademark hair.

Grace Kelly, the original cool blond and muse to the creative genius, director Alfred Hitchcock stared in three of his classic movies. She was gloriously exquisite in the 1955 movie, *To Catch a Thief.* Cary Grant and Grace Kelly were a pairing by Alfred Hitchcock of unparalleled good taste a combination of both beauty and sophistication. In the movie Grace Kelly's definitive, shimmering blond page boy was stunning played against the dazzling location of the French Riviera, and the fabulous diamonds she wore around her neck. In the background of the two actors was a scene where a fireworks display was exploding and igniting as were the two actors on silver screen. It was difficult to decide which to look at and what to admire because it was all so superb. Grace Kelly the future Princess of Monaco was a trend setter of enormous proportions to women everywhere. She added the word class to the fashion vocabulary.

Other images of hair we would follow and duplicate would be Farrah Fawcett's long, luxurious mane of hair. Her iconic poster was the gold standard for selling a record breaking 20 million copies in 1976. Farrah's hair was heavily frosted, then flipped up at the ends framing her face. Her hair style was quite novel and exciting at the time. Hair today is cut frequently angled around the face that way and called face framing. Millions of hair-stylists then would copy Farrah's look so we could all have her same hairdo and feel better about "who we were".

Olympic gold medalists and ice skating champion Dorothy Hamills iconic brilliant trademark haircut was called" the wedge." The haircut was cut with such precision and balance that it enhanced the movement of her spiral turns on the ice. Women everywhere wanted that style in 1976 and still do today.

After two decades people still are talking about and wanting Jennifer Aniston's haircut "the Rachel" wore on the iconic television show *Friends*.

Twiggy, my personal favorite hair icon, wore her hair extremely short and whipped back behind her ears; showing more of her face. Her trademark eyes were made famous by her painted on lashes right below the water line, they were startling when seen- staring at us from the pages and covers of *Vogue*! Twiggy also gave us the confidence to wear our hair short. When we were walking down the street we hoped and felt we resembled her a little.

In 1961, a stunning image appeared at the opening scene of a movie to top all openings of a movie. It was a perfect collaboration of fashion designers, make-up artists, hair stylists, camera men, musicians, song writer, screenwriters, directors all working together on the one and only Audrey Hepburn.

The scene begins without dialogue with music heard from a single harmonica playing the title song *Moon River*. There is an unusual absence of the frenetic traffic from the New York City streets. Only one lone yellow taxi is visible cruising at the early hours of dawn, depositing the lovely Audrey

Hepburn at her destination on Fifth Avenue. She is wearing an elegant formal evening ensemble, a long black column adorned with pearls, exquisite in its simplicity. The ironic sunglasses she is wearing complete the contrasting image of her glamourous formal evening wear in the early morning rising sun. Instead of the obligatory evening purse she carries a brown paper bag in her hands. Slowly she removes the contents and delicately pulls out a cup filled with coffee and a pastry. More symphonic instruments are added and play in the background and there she stands, Audrey Hepburn in all her grace and beauty viewed by us through the stores glass window and she is mesmerizing as Holly Golightly having her *Breakfast at Tiffany's.*

After that one isolated moment in the movie everything else after is anti-climactic.

Any dictionary would define the word "elegant" with just her name Audrey Hepburn. She wore the perfect black dress designed by fashion designer Givenchy, the iconic pearl necklace dangling down her back, her hair was fashioned in an amazing French twist, flawless makeup, the classic sunglasses, all blended together and made even more magical by the music written by Henry Mancini, at the landmark Tiffany's on Fifth Avenue, New York. The irresistible scene carved out indelibly on celluloid for millions to view forever. There will never be another movie scene like it because there will never be another Audrey Hepburn.

It was an artistic achievement, eternal in its beauty that resonates through time; a moment where art meets art in its excellence.

I feel lucky to have lived at the same time as some of those extraordinary icons. Those fabulous women taught us a lot about elegance and style.

Audrey Hepburn, the ultimate "chicster", Grace Kelly, the cool blond, Marilyn Monroe, the ultimate blond sex symbol, Jackie Kennedy, the elegant sophisticate, and Ingrid Bergman – "Here's looking at you." I bid them a silent "thank you" to the memory of their loveliness.

The fact is we are all celebrities of our own worlds. Our image is just as important as a famous star, to our families, friends, coworkers and the people who love us and see us each day. Hair is a major tool in our arsenal for creating an image to be admired, loved and followed just like the stars we venerate in the popular culture.

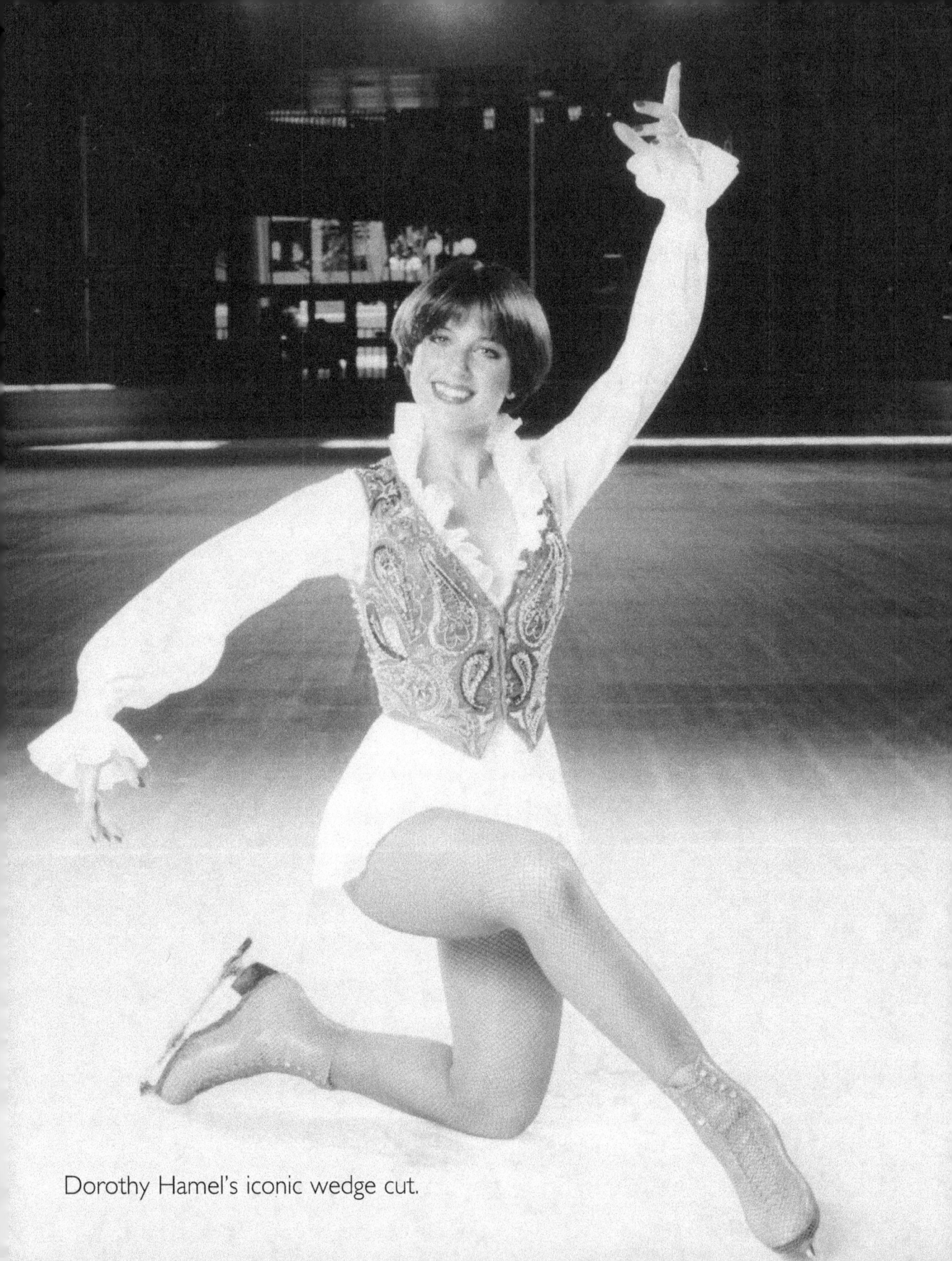

Dorothy Hamel's iconic wedge cut.

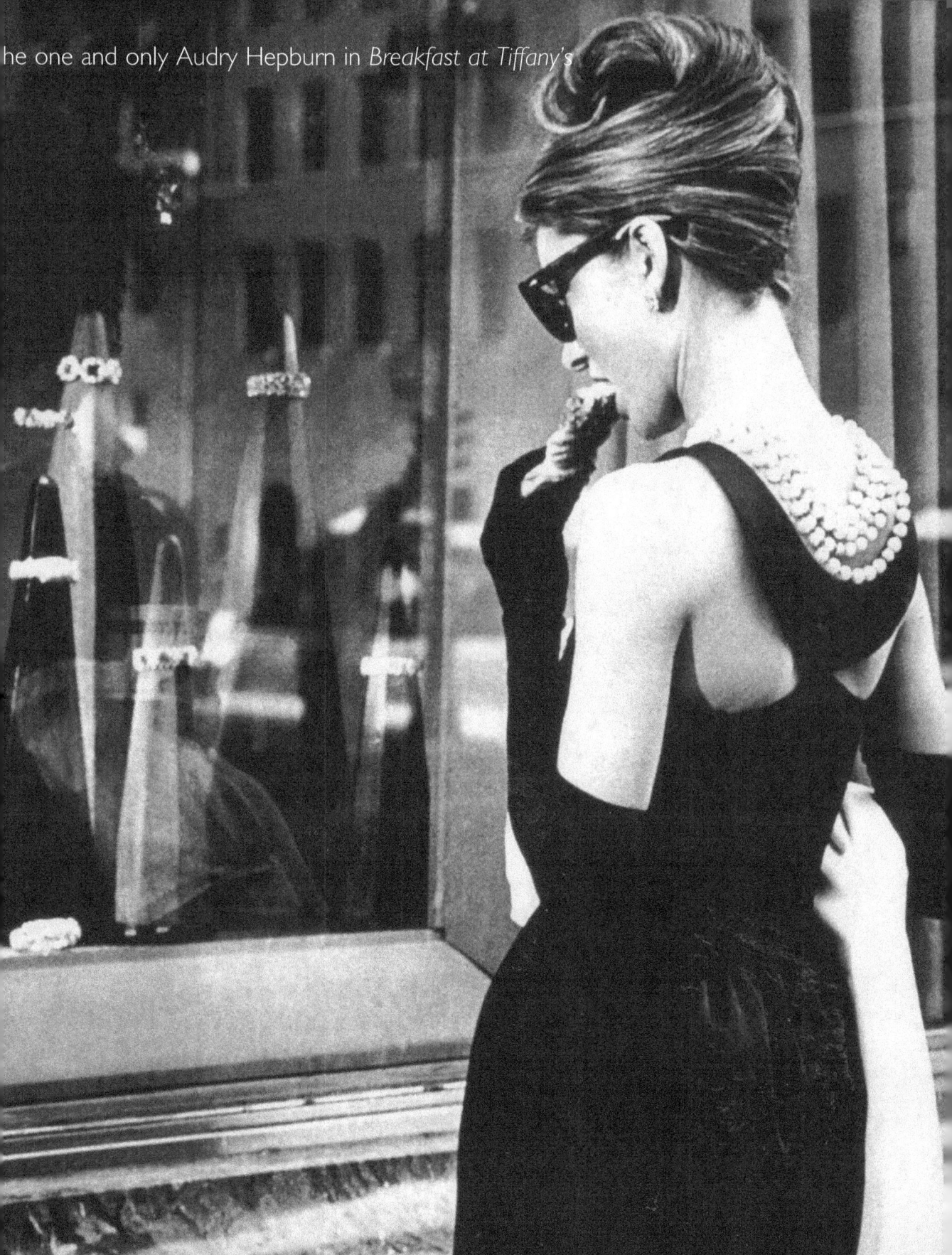

the one and only Audry Hepburn in *Breakfast at Tiffany's*

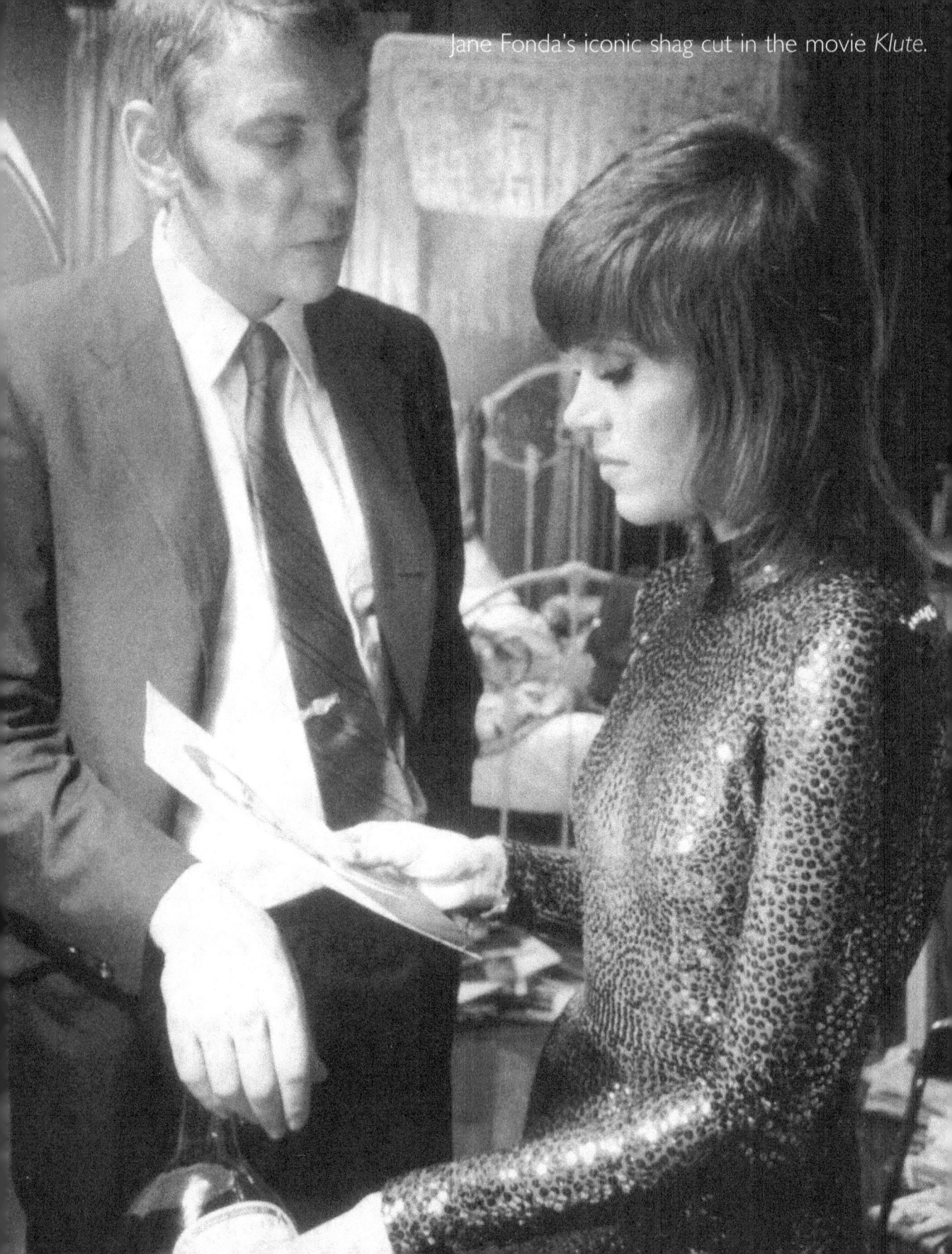

CHAPTER 11
THE ENVELOPE, PLEASE

"Hooray for Hollywood
You may be homely in your neighborhood
But if you think that you can be an actor, see Mr. Factor"

From the film *Hollywood Hotel,* 1937
Johnny Mercer / Richard Whiting

I love the movies. They are an extraordinary art form that encompasses a collaboration of artists coming together to make a visual experience. A film entertains, stirs our emotions visually and can leave a lasting impression by the story it tells.

Hair in a movie can help tell the story. The blending of a character played by the actor and the hair style worn can come together seamlessly and merge the two into one. Each enhances the other's performance in a film. When this collaboration happens in a movie, it can make the actor and the portrayal of the character more relevant and memorable.

Hair can be the star of the film. A perfect example of this phenomenon is the 1989 movie *Klute* with Jane Fonda. Jane Fonda played a prostitute in the film named Bree Daniels. Jane's haircut was called the "Shag" and everyone went crazy over this razor cut. Thirty five years later, the look is still current. Would the movie be as good without Jane Fonda wearing the "shag cut"? For me, the hair was the star of the show.

The Motion Picture Academy has never given an award for this art form. The category would be for exceptional hair in a movie. The award would be

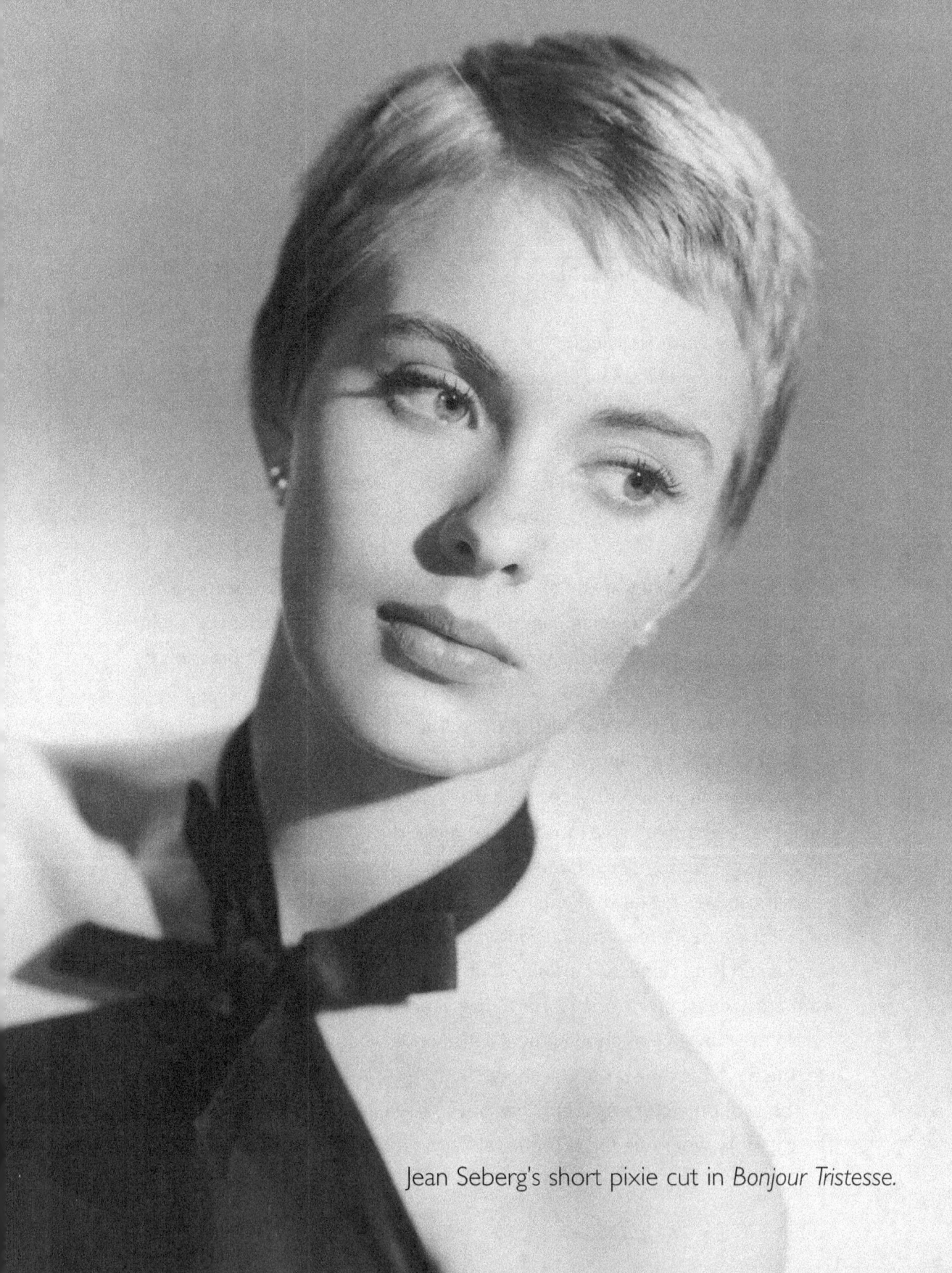

Jean Seberg's short pixie cut in *Bonjour Tristesse*.

given to the professional who created outstanding hair for the character in the film. Who would you pick for great hair in a movie? My nominations for best hair in a film would be as follows; the envelope, please.

The 1958 movie, *Bonjour Tristesse* starring, Jean Seberg would have to be the next recipient for outstanding hair in a film. The character she plays is Cecile, a gamine sprite, who is running around the French Riviera in shorts, bathing suits and Parisian couture gowns by Givenchy and Hermes.

Cecile's hair was cut in an extremely short chic pixie, quite daring for the times. It was very French and stunning, enhancing the features of Jean Seberg's face. The simplicity of the haircut was just the right counterpoint for the designer formal gowns she wore as well as with her casual dresses and bathing suits. Not one hair on her head changed for any of the fashionable outfits she wore except perhaps a change of earrings, and it was stellar. Jean Seberg's hair was the "scene stealer" no one else could compare standing next to her. Watching the movie, I couldn't keep my eyes from following her image and no one else's across the wide screen. Every time I see the film, Jean Seberg always leaves me *Breathless.*

Sometimes I watch a movie just to see the hair in it. I have composed a short list of favorites from the many iconic portrayals of hair from the movies. How the actor's hair was styled helped to enhance and define the character more and made the performance more memorable.

Can there be a more beloved character then Julie Andrews as Maria in 1965 film *The Sound of Music?* Her apron and haircut endeared us to her image for generations to love and admire spanning over six decades. Can you imagine Maria singing on the hill tops of Austria in a ponytail or extensions? Her haircut is a distinct entity not to be separated from Julie Andrews or Maria Von Trapp in the movie. Her hair style has become a unique trademark

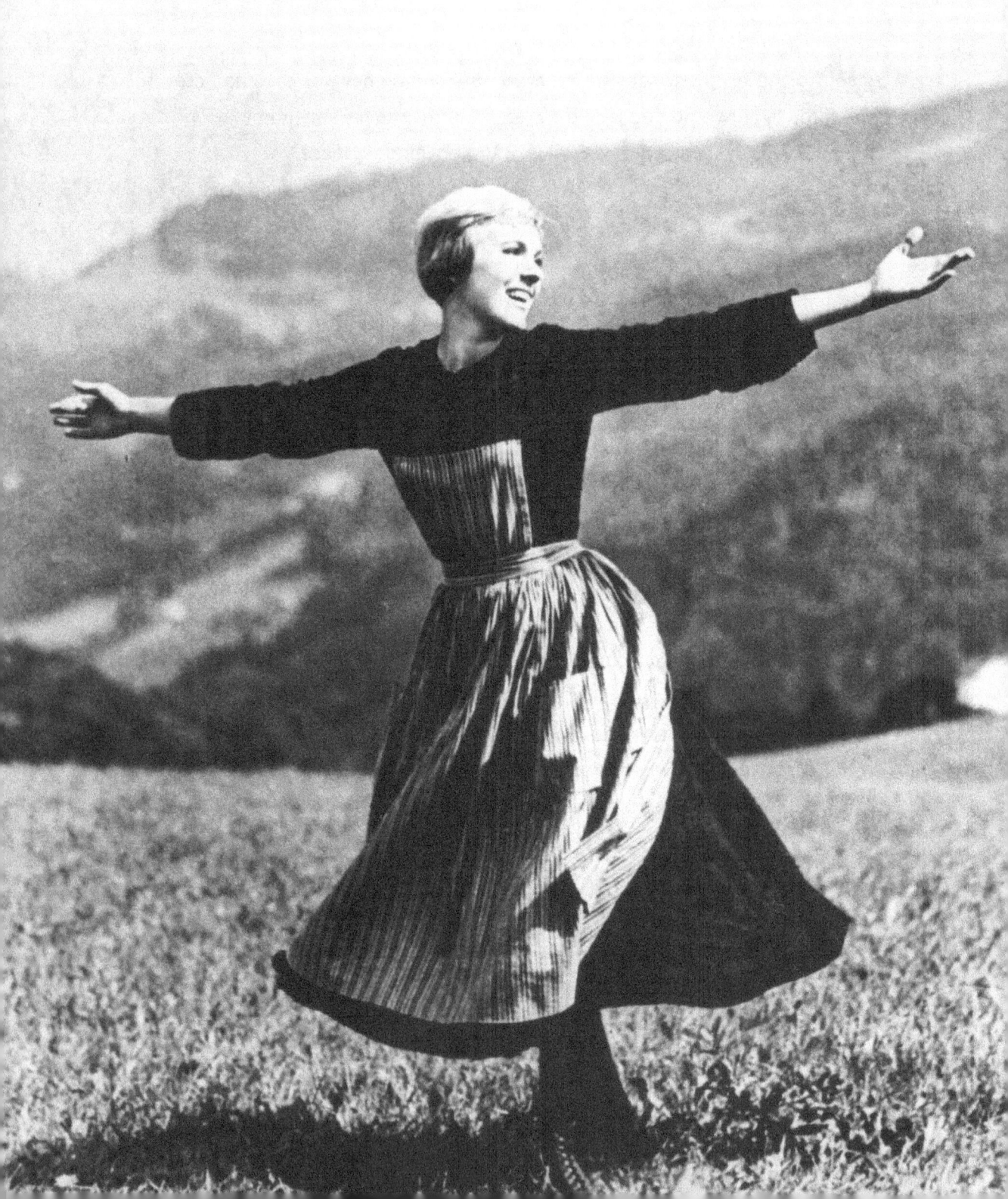

Julie Andrews' iconic hairstyle in *The Sound of Music*.

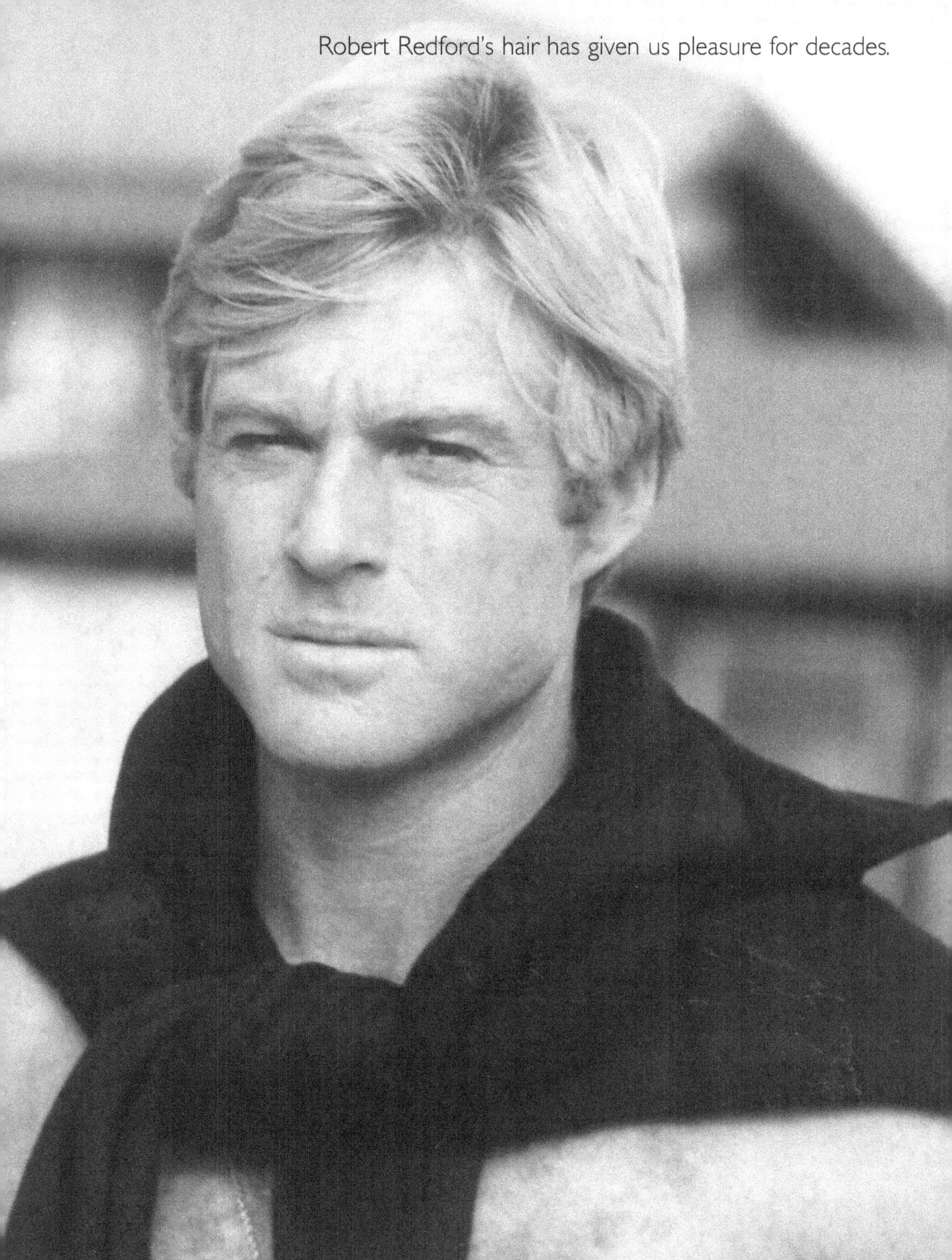

Robert Redford's hair has given us pleasure for decades.

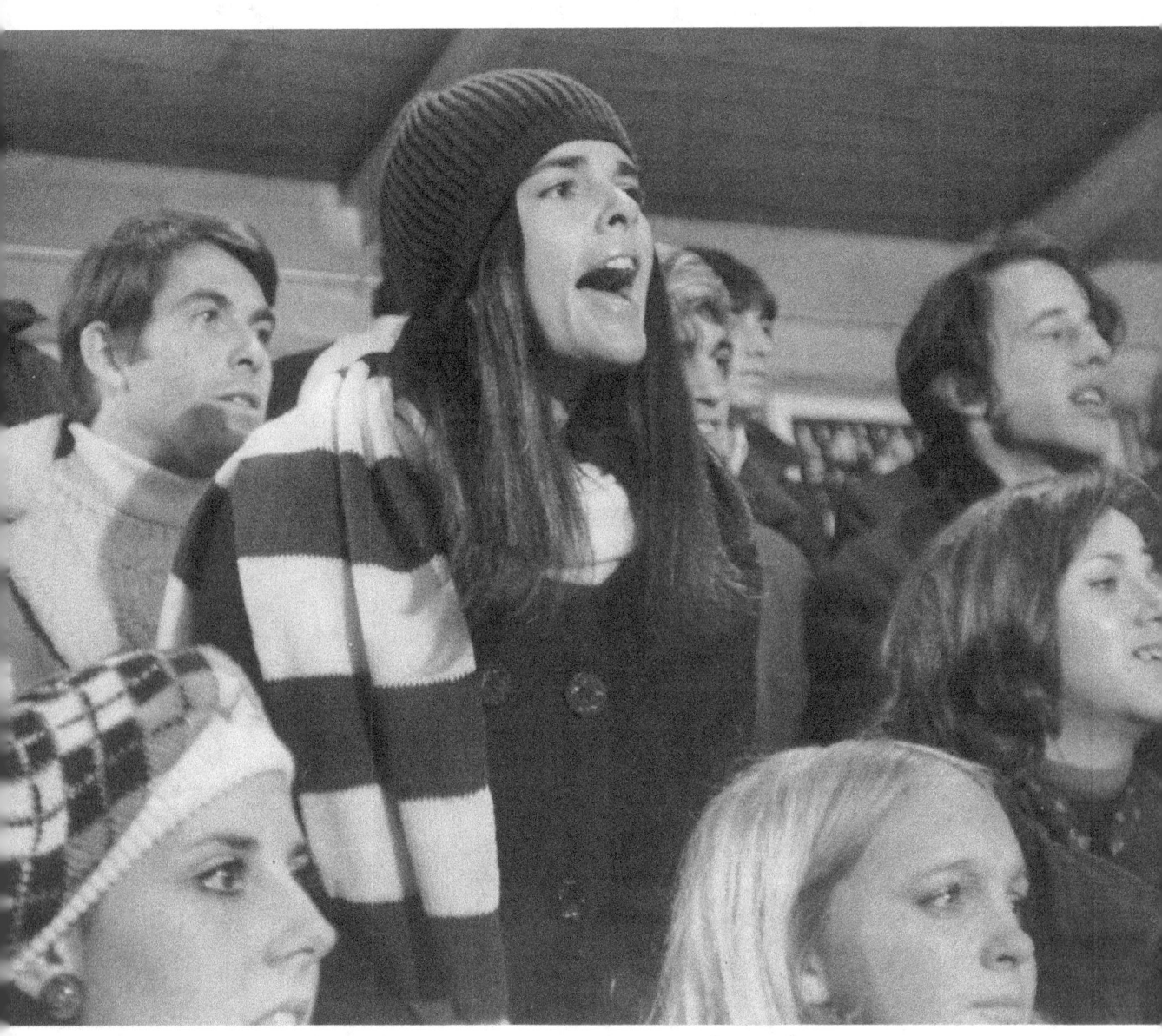

Ali MacGraw

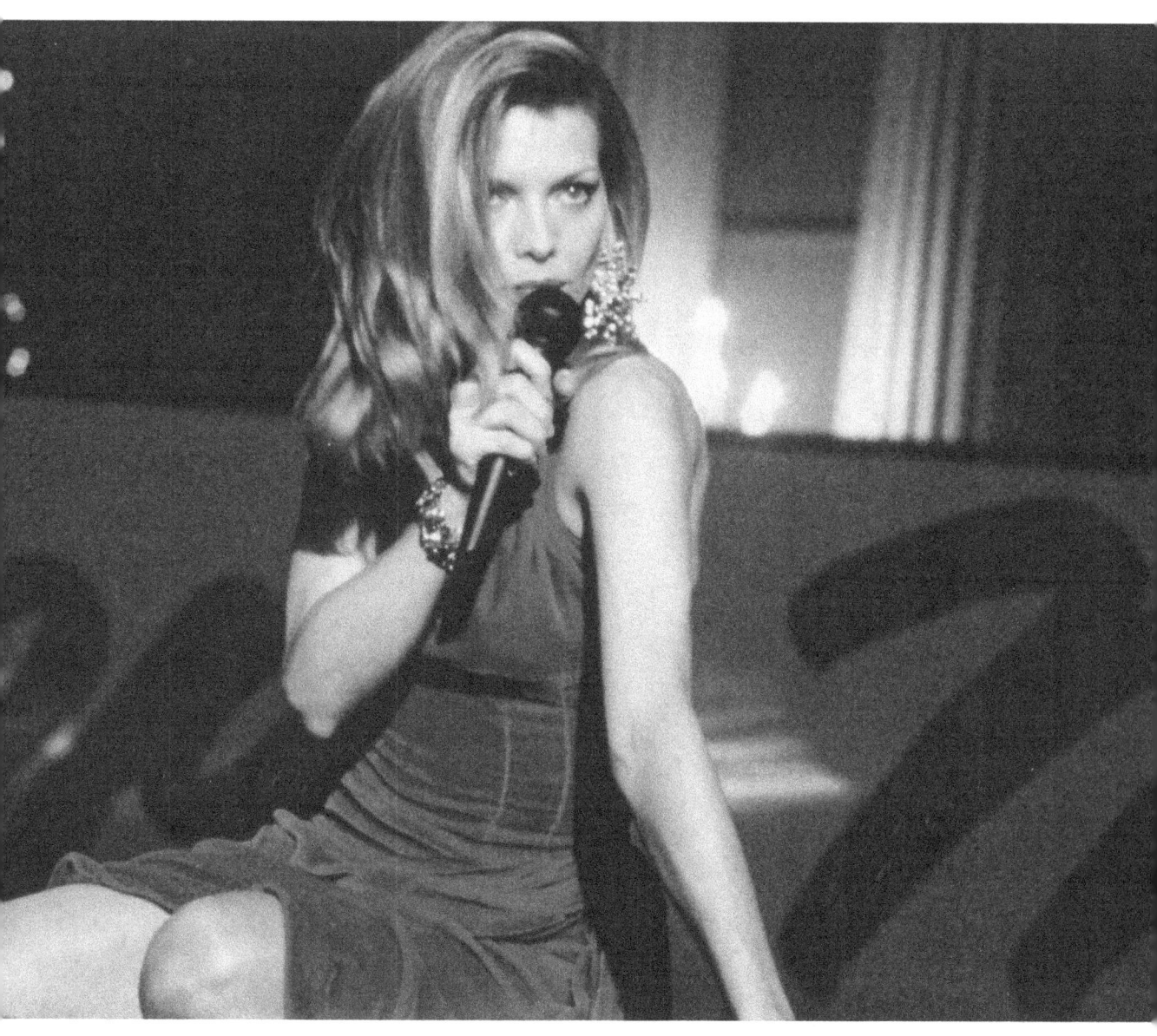

Michelle Pfeiffer

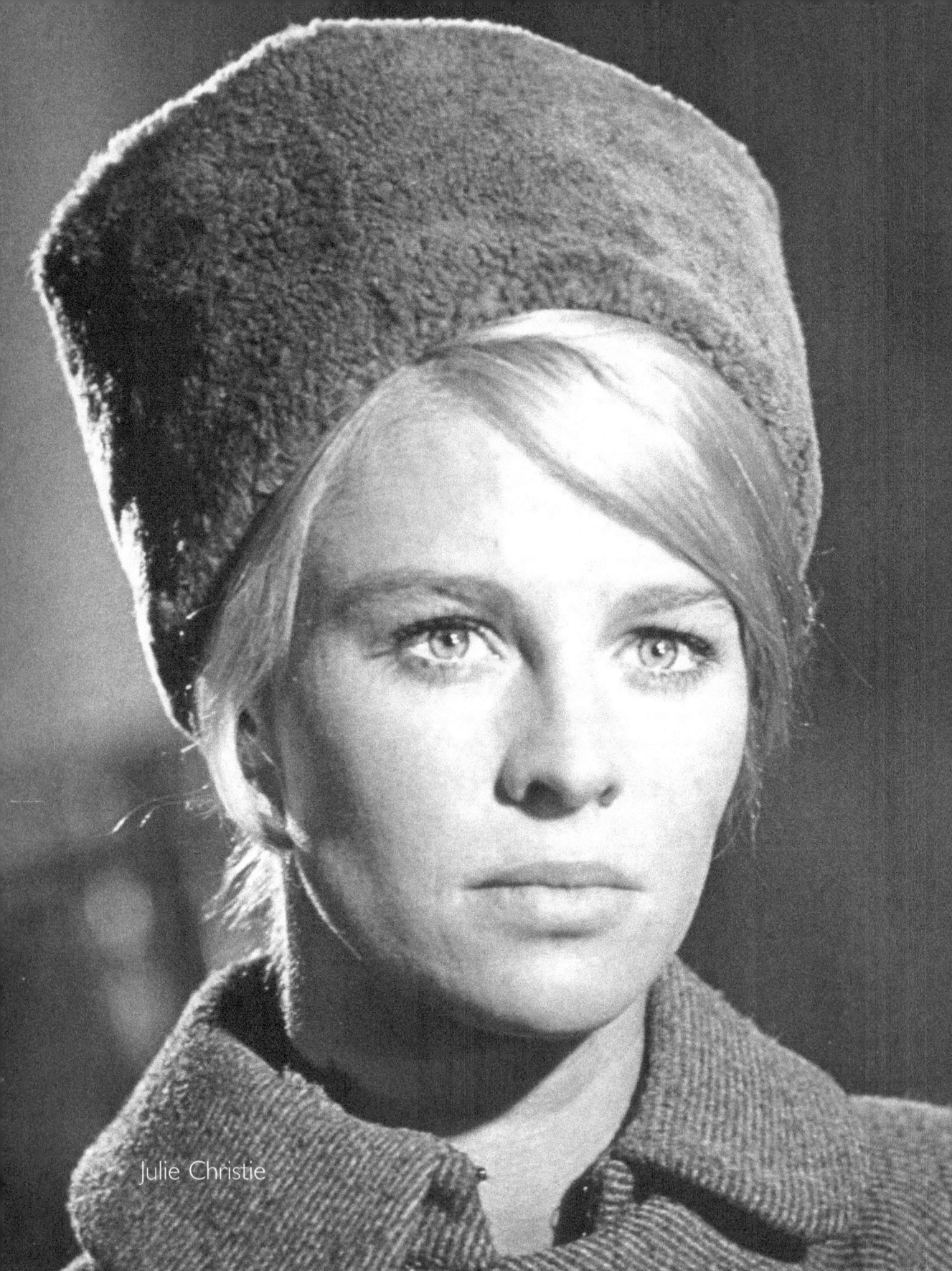

Julie Christie

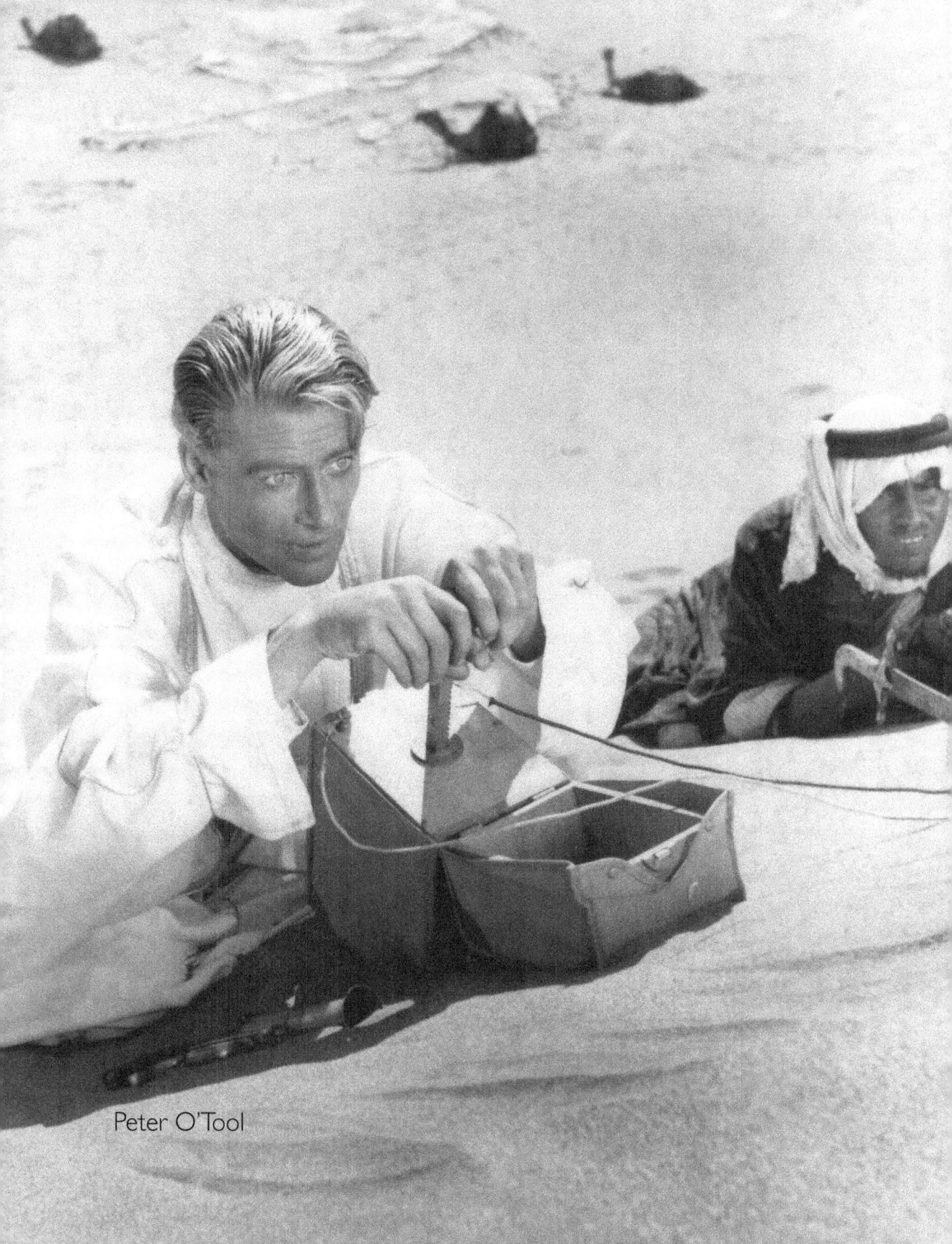
Peter O'Tool

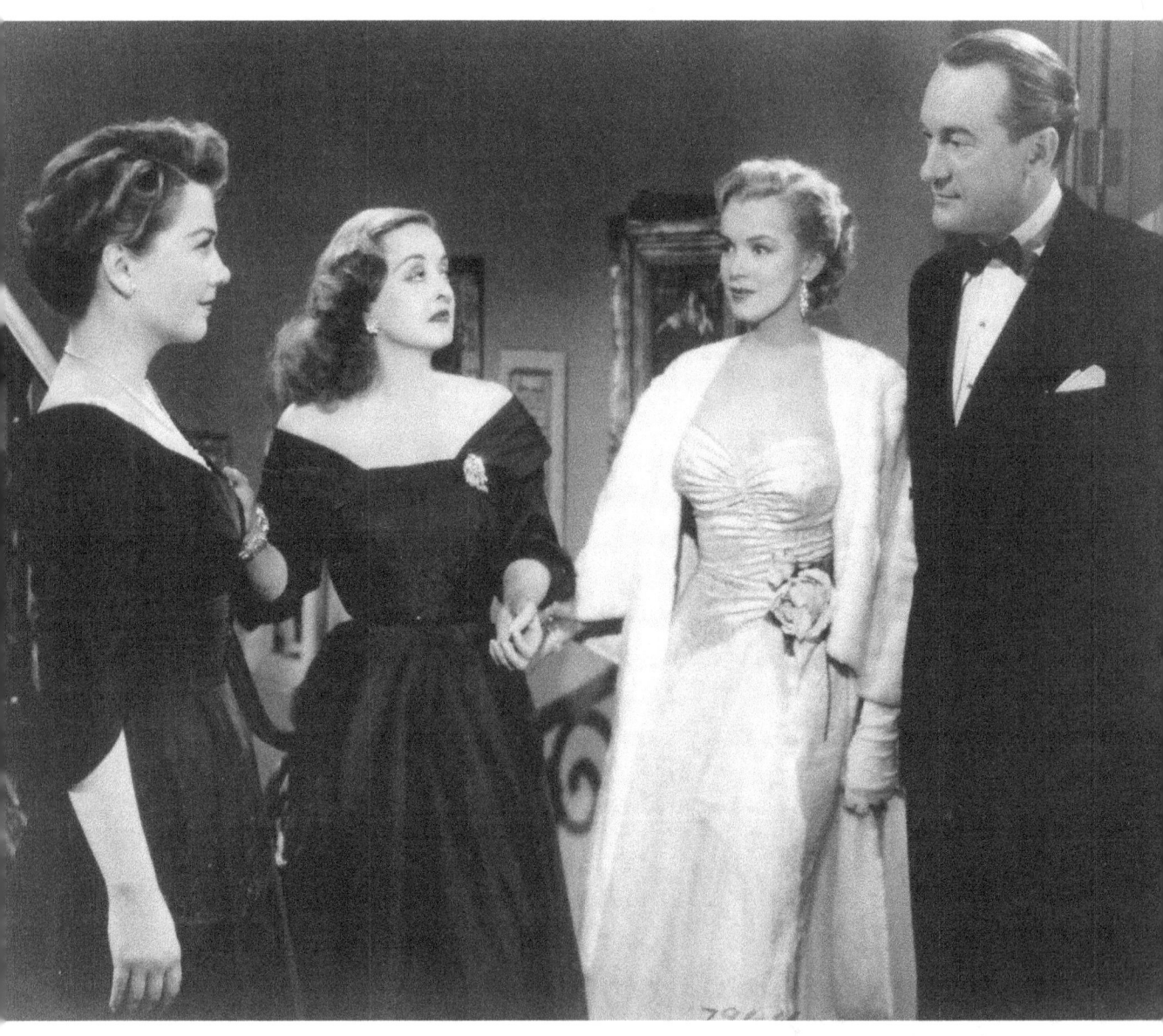

Bette Davis; "Fasten your set belts."

of Julie Andrews and the character, Maria, following them both for an entire lifetime.

Another nominee for great hair in a movie is Ali MacGraw's hair in the 1970's *Love Story*. Her beautiful long shiny tresses are styled with a center part exposing her fabulous eyebrows. Actually, those brows may be the real star of the film. My favorite look in the film is when Jenny Cavilleri played by Ali is wearing the wool knit cap pulled down over the forehead just grazing her brows. She is wearing a navy blue pea coat, and the style is still a classic!

Michelle Pfeiffer's hair in the 1989 *Fabulous Baker Boys* sizzles as Suzie Diamond. Certainly her moment is when she sings the song, *Making Whoopee* lounging across the top of a grand piano stunning in her red dress. A gorgeous hair moment! Her hair throughout the film was consistently more fabulous then those Baker boys, although Jeff Bridges hair was pretty fabulous as well.

If there is an award to be given for outstanding hair color in a movie it would have to be given to Julie Christie in the movie, *Dr. Zhivago*. Her hair in every scene emanates light that looks celestial. The blond hair contrasts with her skin tone and eyes, one enhancing the other. The Russian scenery and other amazing actors are in the film but Julie Christie's hair stands alone as a major player in the film. Omar Sharif could also pick up a nomination for the best mustache in a film.

Actually Peter O Toole's hair color and style dazzles us in the movie, *Lawrence of Arabia.* He and his hair are the magnificent foil when he burns his officer's uniform in the Arabian dessert and dons the Arab robes. Peter O Toole is glorious in the movie and the spectacular musical score written for the film by Maurice Jarre is equal to the image of Peter O Toole riding across the desert.

An award could also be given to the most consistently superb hair on a male in films and the statuette must go to the brilliant Robert Redford: The 1973 movie, *The Way We Were,* Barbara Streisand pushing away the golden lock of hair from Hubbell Gardiners forehead in an intimate gesture of love from the movie—always a thril. Or his amazing hair in the unforgettable *All the President's Men, The Candidate,* and *Butch Cassidy and the Sundance Kid.* Whoever is responsible for his haircuts I am deeply appreciative because it is always on the money. His hair continuously stars in any Robert Redford film and always gives pleasure to look at over the decades in performance after performance.

If I had to pick an award for the best hairstyle on an actor in a movie, I would have to go back to the black and white films of the forties. Nothing since that period can match the romance, drama and mystery of those films and the women in them. If you're not familiar these actresses of this genre, you have not experienced star power.

Ingrid Bergman was luminous in *Casablanca* 1942. Greer Garson in *Mrs. Miniver* or *Random Harvest* was supreme. The glorious Gene Tierney in the movie *Laura*, also the 1944 film *Leave Her to Heaven,* is at the height of her beauty. Jennifer Jones wild sensuous hair style in the 1947 movie, *Duel in the Sun*, her hair spoke volumes about the character she played in the film. Do yourself a favor on a rainy afternoon. Get to know these films and these women; it's a gift you can give to yourself.

One hair moment does stand out among the many. The best hair in a feature film would go to Bette Davis in *All about Eve*, 1950. She is older in the film but like fine wine aged wonderfully. Bette Davis' hair is full and extravagant with lustrous waves falling to her shoulders. Without that hair her role in the film would be seriously compromised.

Bette Davis plays Margo Channing in the movie. She is giving a cocktail party in her Manhattan apartment for her lover, who was played by Gary Merrill. Margo is a successful Broadway actress. Her boyfriend, Bill Samson, is a theater director in New York and is giving way too much attention to Margo's younger protégé, Eve Harrington, at the party. Quite peeved, Ms. Davis enters the room in a fabulous, taffeta, cocktail dress by the academy-award winning fashion designer Edith Head. Taffeta is a beautiful and shiny material that is quite noisy when you move in it. It does add drama when worn on the body. Taffeta was used a lot in the fifties and sixties for party dresses.

Margo Channing is raging with jealousy while holding a martini in one hand; she then hands her glass over to someone standing at the party in a supreme gesture of defiance. Margo then plans her dramatic exit across the room via another staircase. Her dress swishing loudly, the incomparable Ms. Davis gets to the stairs stops and slowly turns around to face her guests and then in one grand moment says, "Fasten your seat belts; it's going to be a bumpy night".

Seriously that moment is movie history. I have always wanted to say that to someone. There is something about the hair in black and white films that in the right lighting gives a halo effect and it is devastating in a movie and is responsible for those movie moments to be more magnetic.

In the collaboration of a film, not any one person can take full credit. There is a combined effort of a community: the actors, set director, musicians, cameramen, writers, director, producers; fashion designer, makeup artists, and hair stylist all contribute.

I would like to present the award for best hair in a film and the recipient would be Gladys Witten the hair stylist responsible for Bette Davis' hair in the movie, *All about Eve.* The hair style is still as current and relevant today as it was sixty years before. Her hair and character in the film are one, seamless each contributing to the others performance.

Over the decades much praise and appreciation should go to all the creative hair stylists that have the imagination and artistry to make the men and women we love to watch in the movies, love them more.

There was a time you could only watch a film in a movie theater. When the movie changed or left your city it was never available to be seen again, it vanished and was gone. You might get another chance to see it if played again randomly on one of the four television stations.

Then, in 1976, the inventor of the Video cassette, James T Russell, made movies available for us to view in our homes. That DVD and its requisite player changed everything and made it possible for us to view these beloved films at any time. These movies are a time capsule captured from the imagination and creative efforts of so many artists. Their work can live on for generations to appreciate their struggles, passion and spirit for their artistry are an inspiration.

Hair has a language that speaks,

To understand hairs'
language, you must
listen with your eyes.………

Cosmetology School

CHAPTER 12
HAIR:
A METAPHOR FOR CHANGE

"Ch-ch-ch-ch - Changes
(Turn and face the strain)
Ch-ch - Changes"

David Bowie

The previous chapters were written as a star struck admirer of hair through most of the decades of my life. In 2008 my perspective on these grand strands would change dramatically. From an observer to an active participant, I would become a professional hairstylist. I would learn to cut, color, and style, straighten and perm these wondrous threads of protein. I would now be doing hair on others instead of the spectator sport I so enjoyed. The transition would lead me down a road I never expected.

The path would diverge into a much deeper meaning of what hair would represent to my life and force me on an inner journey as well as take me on a ride of spiritual truth. This transformation would be a sojourn of psychological and spiritual proportions that eventually lead me to writing this story.

I was a successful interior designer for thirty years. At one time I owned two retail furniture stores. I witnessed a change in this business when the corporations and the Internet started to undermine small individual owned businesses and causing them to disappear. The buying power of a large chain of stores cannot be equal in the market to a small business owner. People started shopping for furniture and buying on line and corporate owned furniture stores mailed appetizing, glossy catalogs to every home in America.

San Francisco's iconic furniture mart on Market Street slowly closed their doors to furniture showrooms and opened its doors to the offices of high tech firms. San Francisco always hosted a winter and summer furniture market for years. It was a time honored tradition where people traveled from different cities to buy and sell their products. We would climb the buses that were provided and they would take us to the various destinations to view all the latest innovations in the design world. My partner Charlie and I along with our employees would look forward to this event each year. It was an opportunity to see old friends and all the suppliers we did business with. Alas, this too has disappeared with regret and fond memories.

A chapter closed for me in interior design and a new journey began. I started to think about a new career in 2008.

If you delay a decision too long you might become paralyzed by the choice at hand. Fear and anxiety may visit and become much too comfortable with you. After much agonizing I realized that fear, and anxiety of being older was delaying me from moving forward in a new career choice.

With great panic and excitement, I signed up at the east bay Paul Mitchell The School for cosmetology when I was sixty two years of age. Hair would now be a metaphor for change in my life. Starting a new career after thirty years of design was going to be hard, and learning new skills in my sixties was going to be a challenge. The student body was an impossibly young culture and so were the teachers. I was going to have to overcome so many obstacles within myself that later would prove to be my greatest assets.

The first of which was my ageing brain. Short term memory lapses required reconnecting synapses and nerve endings to learn new concepts and ideas to make the new information stick. I also had to face the challenge of joining a youthful culture of tattoos and piercings, and not be critical or judgmental of them or, they of me. Eventually I also had to fight the inclination to get a tattoo for myself at the back of my neck.

I tried to understand the lyrics of their music and rap that was played all day long, when all I wanted to hear was Vivaldi's *Four Seasons* or Frank Sinatra while I was learning to highlight and roll perms.

As I am getting older, photographs and mirrors are not enjoyable and like a vampire that hates the daylight, I try to avoid them both whenever possible. In beauty schools and salons, unhappily, mirrors are everywhere and the lighting is also unbearable. In some lighting you can look completely bald standing in the right position.

I drank less coffee in the morning because the caffeine was making my hand shake while holding the scissors. Usually I ate alone at lunch and breaks. Most of the time, I was feeling invisible and irrelevant, but I did learned to listen more. The veins in my legs were painful and engorged from standing the eight hours each day. But I persevered. My motto, like Winston Churchill's KBO in World War Two, brought me new meaning. I was going to "Keep Buggering On."

Then magic started to happen...

I began to see the uniqueness of each student and fall in love with each one more each day. I listened to their stories and then began worrying about them.

When we were tested, I surprisingly passed the tests and began to feel exhilaration and pride at overcoming the obstacles of old age and self-doubt.

I would laugh to myself when a young male guest came in on a Saturday for a haircut and was hoping to get one of the beautiful young girls and instead got me to cut his hair. The look of disappointment on his face soon disappeared when he liked how he looked after his haircut.

Or when I was new on the clinic floor and a guest was delighted with the outcome of the service I had to stop myself from paying their bill and giving them a generous gratuity.

Every day I appeared younger; beauty school was actually the best cosmetic treatment. I finally graduated without missing a day of school with cheers from my fellow classmates. With pride and a heavy dose of great joy I got through it. Passing state board would be the next obstacle to tackle.

Again fear and panic came to visit me. After a lot of hard work I nervously passed, shaking all the way through the state board examiners test. I was then offered a job to stay on at the school and work my way up to being an educator, adding more trainings and certifications. I thought I was finished taking exams but I was now furthering my education in preparation for a new career in the industry being an educator. Teaching was the most fulfilling job I've ever had linking me to my true identity.

I learned as an instructor at cosmetology school how to really love without borders or judgments a love that nurtures and makes things grow and develop. The message was to teach and educate the students with love, to inspire students and give them confidence. It wasn't about me anymore it was about them, the students, always them. Helping them to succeed was the most important value I could give. Every day they received the very best of me nothing less. The students of my heart I walk around with them inside of me every day. And when they left and graduated from school, I would never forget them and they knew that. Some people say when you're ready to leave this planet you can't take anything with you; well, I say you can and its love, always love. Hair became my teacher and taught me new lessons that enhanced my life.

CHAPTER 13
COSMETOLOGY SCHOOL

"Come on people now
Smile on your brother
Everybody get together
Try to love one another
Right now"

-THE YOUNGBLOODS-

I started cosmetology school as a student and eventually became an instructor. I learned new skills but I learned much more than cutting and coloring hair. The very best part of school was the melting pot of different ethnic cultures; a cauldron bubbling over with great diversity of ages and religions working together under one roof. When students and teachers were working together on projects with one another this dance of differences made us one, and we were all the same. We were equal in our passion and desire to give our best to the guest, ourselves and the fellow student we were working and sharing the service with.

The very act of washing a stranger's hair creates an intimacy and trust between two people. Running your fingers through the scalp of someone from a different culture different from your own breaks barriers and that is a powerful experience. Maybe that's what Christ had in mind in the Bible when he washed the feet of his disciples. The very act washes us clean spiritually; maybe it could have been hair?

My experience at cosmetology school has led me to believe hair can be a metaphor for peace. Here is an idea and proposal for a solution to bring world Peace among nations. It's a formula all political leaders and governments can follow. Any individual who has difficulty with the diversity of cultures, and religions that are different from their own, or are upset by the sexual preferences of other people would benefit by the idea.

Send the world leaders to Cosmetology School. Let them spend a year learning to cut hair, highlight, color, and roll perms. Make these politicians, join the students to learn and work together at a beauty school. It will be a step in the direction towards world peace. I realize this is a fantasy, but when reading this try to visualize the world leaders working behind the chairs of a beauty school working on hair services. Like all humor there runs a serious truth.

Through this shared experience leaders can find commonality with each other and build respect, even if their ideologies' are different. Learning to work together could eliminate what divides us and together build a positive connection.

The Student Body:

The student body of this fictitious school should consist of world leaders from foreign countries mixed with students from a diversity cultures: Hispanic, African American, Asian, Indian, Middle Eastern, and Caucasian. Also there would be different religions and belief systems as well as a variety of sexual preferences.

This melting pot is predominately young and just out of high school .There is a possibility of a few older students making career changes and they can complement and bring experience and nurturance to the rest of the student population. Some students may be dealing with depression, anger and low self-esteem. Others have experienced abuse and neglect and some are recovering from serious addictions. Emotions run high and fast in this wide-ranging and passionate population.

A bully (hopefully not more than one) and a couple of prom queens enrich the brew of dissimilarities and attitudes. Huge complications can occur. Fights, slurs and jealousies might interfere and preventing the stability of the students from liking each other and working together.

Among the student population, some might be pregnant, while others are already single mothers with babies; some married, or divorced, others engaged. A proportion is nursing a broken heart and in need of healing while others are happily in love. All types of emotional experiences can increase the obstacles and volatility of every day. If this group can fuse, and find a way to get along together, then I believe most any country can. The creative passion and desire to succeed is the glue which holds all the multiplicities together.

The Mission Statement:

Every day on the clinic floor of Cosmetology school, there are difficult projects to work on. These services, like highlights and color corrections require skill and patience. You have to sometimes partner and work with a fellow student whether you like them or not to complete the required service. Working together on a difficult assignment makes you forget the insignificant things and focus on what's really essential; like finishing the task at hand without damaging the client's hair.

The team you were assigned hopefully will help you achieve successful results. Together your teacher, student partner and most importantly the guest sitting in the chair are there to support you. Unfortunately, your guest thought she would be finished much earlier and is anxious to leave and is now giving you dirty looks in the mirror and is looking at her watch anxiously. You're starting to sweat and get very nervous but having a partner to work with is a great help in calming the tension.

Working with another student on a challenging project will build the confidence needed when you are doing the service alone. Meanwhile you are not alone. There is someone to help and share the failures as well as the rewards with you and that goes a long way in building friendship.

The Program:

If one of the world leaders is feeling more superior then the others, he must immediately start the arrogant leader highlighting a guest. Start him early in the morning and make sure the guest he is working on has super long hair that is very wavy with gray roots. Make sure they are using horizontal quarter inch sectioning. Make him take the weaving comb and start lifting each strand in a pick up two and drop two rhythms. Have him apply the lightener to the foils very carefully and fold so the bleach won't bleed on the remaining hair. In between the foil, be certain he brushes on the hair color and applies it alternately as to cover the gray near the scalp.

You will be standing in one place for several hours and may have done seventy foils, the work is tedious and you will probably miss lunch and breaks so I hope you had a good breakfast. Not being experienced at highlighting might take hours so please wear comfortable shoes. The student helping with the service can take the front while you take the back of the clients head. Five hours is not unusual for first time highlighters.

After the rinse they may need to tone and that's an extra step that will require more time. Then a cut and a blow dry. You are tired from standing in one spot all day and all you want to do is sit down in a chair and eat. Hopefully, your partner who helped you will stay and help with the blow dry because you're starving.

By this time the student and world leader have become great friends telling stories from each ones country and sharing the fatigue together. The help was appreciated and a bond is forged. You both are humbled by the shared experience and a friendship now grows where one did not exist before. It really didn't matter what your partner's race or religion was, all you know is you were grateful for the help and you know could not have done it without each other.

I know the "secret" to World Peace:

The very next morning another guest with long black hair wants to be platinum blond. Her texture is fine with heavy density. This is a very difficult service and being alert and on damage control is crucial. Again, students and politicians have to work as a team and you must work quickly with speed and maximum communication between partners. You're up to your elbows in bleach and even if you were not fond of or liked each other before the service, by the time you finish the service you will.

Another guest is upset with the color she chose and is now blaming you. You know it's not your fault, but you run to the bathroom crying because you think it is and you worked so hard is to make her happy. Alternately the haircut you just finished was cut much shorter than the guest wanted it to be cut and she is now crying in the chair. The North Korean leader, who did the haircut, is feeling bad, and runs to the bathroom in tears. Some students see the distress and run in to help soothe the world leader and someone they never expected to see in the bathroom was the South Korean leader also there to comfort as well. Wow! Suddenly everyone is starting to feel cared for and beginning to feel part of something larger a connection to a community.

Practicing the skills you learned on another student is helpful and also a lot of fun. On the clinic floor you might see the Iraqi leader giving the Iranian leader a much needed haircut and a Taliban fighter is finally getting his toes cut and polished by an Afghan. The President of the United States is coloring the Russian leader's hair purple, and if the President's wife likes the color, she will book an appointment with him next week. The leader from China and the Tibetan leader are in a deep consultation and asking advice on a cut and color and they are both going to lunch together after the service is complete.Across the room in a faraway corner the Israeli and Palestinian leaders are rolling perms and folding foils together. Lately the gestures of kindness are helping everyone to feel better about each other.

I know the secret to World Peace is to send the leaders of countries to Cosmetology School:

It didn't seem to matter what the cultural differences were or the individual sexualities were when working together. The joint focus of a job well done superseded old prejudices and the comraderies' remained the value to be cherished. Kindnesses are always remembered.

Send world leaders of countries to Cosmetology School. Teach them to cut color and style hair, and on the way to highlight and perm, they just might find a peaceful co-existence.

It can be done. A diversity of people learning and working together can bring a healthy respect for each other and create richness to our respective lives. This truly was the most important lesson I experienced and shared at the time I spent at Cosmetology school. Things didn't always work out perfectly with everyone but the opportunity of appreciation, cooperation and respect was always possible.

I was much older when I graduated from school this time around and it gave me a different perspective by seeing things through the eyes of an older crone.   The wants and needs I thought were important in my youth were stripped down to what is essential. Wisdom, kindness and love are what prevail, Thank Goodness.

CHAPTER 14
TRANSFORMATIONS

"Changing the world begins with the very
 personal process of changing yourself,
 the only place you can begin is where you are,
 and the only time you can begin is always now."

~ Gary Zukav, *Seat of the Soul*

Most people don't like change and it's especially true regarding their hair. Keeping things the way they are, or status quo, is a comfort to them.

There is power in change and it takes courage and risk. The power is being open to try something new and expand your current outlook. You never know the possibilities until you try some of them. When I decorated interiors of rooms, it was the same principle as hair. If you don't change it up now and then, it can become stale and boring. A room can be enhanced by just moving a couch around to a different wall or having it float to the center. There can be a tremendous excitement just by cutting or adding a bang or fringe that never appeared on your forehead before. You can't know the potential of something unless you take a chance.

I was watching an old movie from the early thirties; Lana Turner was a newcomer to Hollywood in the film. I had never seen her with brown hair before. It was amazing to see the change that the platinum blond did to her image. The transformation catapulted her to iconic stature and her stylist might have been responsible for the makeover.

I have been witness to hundreds of transformations and it takes fearless-ness and honesty especially in changing your appearance. The process can yield more then you ever realized. Facing your fear is a challenge but the reward of undertaking the risk is always a great accomplishment to savor. There is a shift in your thinking and your perception has been altered and that is always a gift for your soul.

How to begin the make over? First start with a stylist you trust. Not all hair dressers are the same technically or artistically. In other words, some are better than others.

Next is an appraisal of your face shape. There are eight shapes and a lot of people are unaware of their own face shape. Your next assessment would be your facial features you might want to enhance or diminish. If you have been wearing the same hair style forever, you probably are not aware of your hidden assets. You have ignored your fabulous cheekbones or your jawline and not even been aware of your great eyes. Maybe a bang or fringe would draw more attention to them. Some people really hide in their hair and don't realize that a haircut can actually make them look thinner or years younger.

After an evaluation of the above, it would be helpful to understand your hairs texture. Is your hair curly, wavy or straight? Is the diameter of your hair strand fine medium or coarse? Knowing the texture and the hair density helps make good choices and gives you a realistic approach to the style you want. You need to maintain and duplicate the style when you are on your own and having this information is helpful in achieving successful results.

Maybe color will be part your new look. Checking the temperature of your eye color and skin tone is enormously helpful in choosing the right shade. Are you warm with a yellow undertone or is your eye color leaning towards the cool with blue tints as the tone. Are you in favor of great contrast like black hair with pale skin? Perhaps a blending with less contrast is preferred.

Products also make a huge difference in solving the challenges of certain hair types. Todays' products are so advanced, there is a solution for every issue you can have. Styling tools are another important factor in keeping the style fresh and lasting.

One Saturday morning a client came in with a picture of Jennifer Anniston's wonderful shoulder length bob cut. The highlights in the picture enhanced her haircut, and there was slight layering and some face framing. After a very through consultation the guest said she did not want highlights, and that she would not blow dry her hair, or use a round brush. Styling tools or products would not be an option. She just wanted to get up in the morning and have her hair look like Jennifer Anniston's hair looked in the picture.

Jennifer Anniston does not look like that picture when she gets out of bed in the morning, without the aid of a blow dryer and hair products. Having a realistic expectation does help with the result and less disappointment.

When all the elements are present, as a hair stylist I have witnessed magic. When a makeover is complete, happiness is radiated from every cell and strand. There is a shift in the client's perception of who they think they were and how they are now. Client, stylist and all the others who have been witness to the transformation have been moved sometimes to tears. Everyone is excited by the change and exudes a joyfulness and pride at the result.

Students often ask me "Elayne, what is your favorite movie?" Without hesitation I always answer the 1942 black and white film, *Now Voyager,* starring Bette Davis. Without a doubt it, is the best make over film ever made. Ms. Davis is Charlotte Vail, considered by her family an Old Maid in her mid-thirties and looks in her sixties. Heavy brows, an ancient looking marcel finger waved hairstyle, frumpy dresses and shoes and of course a pair of old fashioned glasses add years to her image.

Charlotte undergoes a huge transformation and is reinvented into an elegant and wildly desirable woman who is sailing on a cruise ship to South America. Eyebrows arched, new do, glassless and designer ensembles of dresses, hats and shoes Charlottes make over is a triumphant success. Destiny brings the actor Paul Henreid on the ship as well and he falls madly in love with the mysterious Charlotte Vail.

The real metamorphosis occurs internally as well as physically. Charlotte Vail is no longer fearful as she once was and a new strength and courage emerge. Her beauty is now in her powerfulness and the ability to overcome her overbearing and domineering mother. She was now free from her fears.

Charlotte Vail in her late thirties finally begins to feel good and confident about herself. The change in her appearance precipitated her internal revelations that fed this dramatic result. The two actions, the outer physical change and the psychological one, produced a new response, each releasing the greater potential of the other. Both brought positive changes resulting in the birth of a new self-assurance and confidence.

The myth or fairytale *Cinderella* has the Fairy Godmother accountable for *Cinderella's* make over. Changing the dress from tattered rags to a beautiful gown and her hair to a new and lovely hairstyle gave Cinderella, like Charlotte Vail the opportunity to transform their feelings of unworthiness to being worthy.

The makeover or transformation had the power to influence and kick start a new self-confidence and start a new inner journey. Perhaps a change in your appearance can inspire a psychological journey that is also needed each linking the one to the other.

As a stylist bringing that kind of happiness to another person is the best feeling and you are so grateful to be part of the experience. You know in that moment at the very core of your being that giving is receiving and they are the same thing. The author of that concept knew that; perhaps Christ was not a carpenter after all; maybe he might have been a hairdresser.

Transformations require openness, faith and trust, honesty, and good communication.

Hopefully, together the hair stylist will have the permission to let the artist inside her bring out the best in you, each honoring the other. Together the creative matrix will give birth to a new image and inspire a new confidence that will be enjoyed every day or at least until the next haircut.

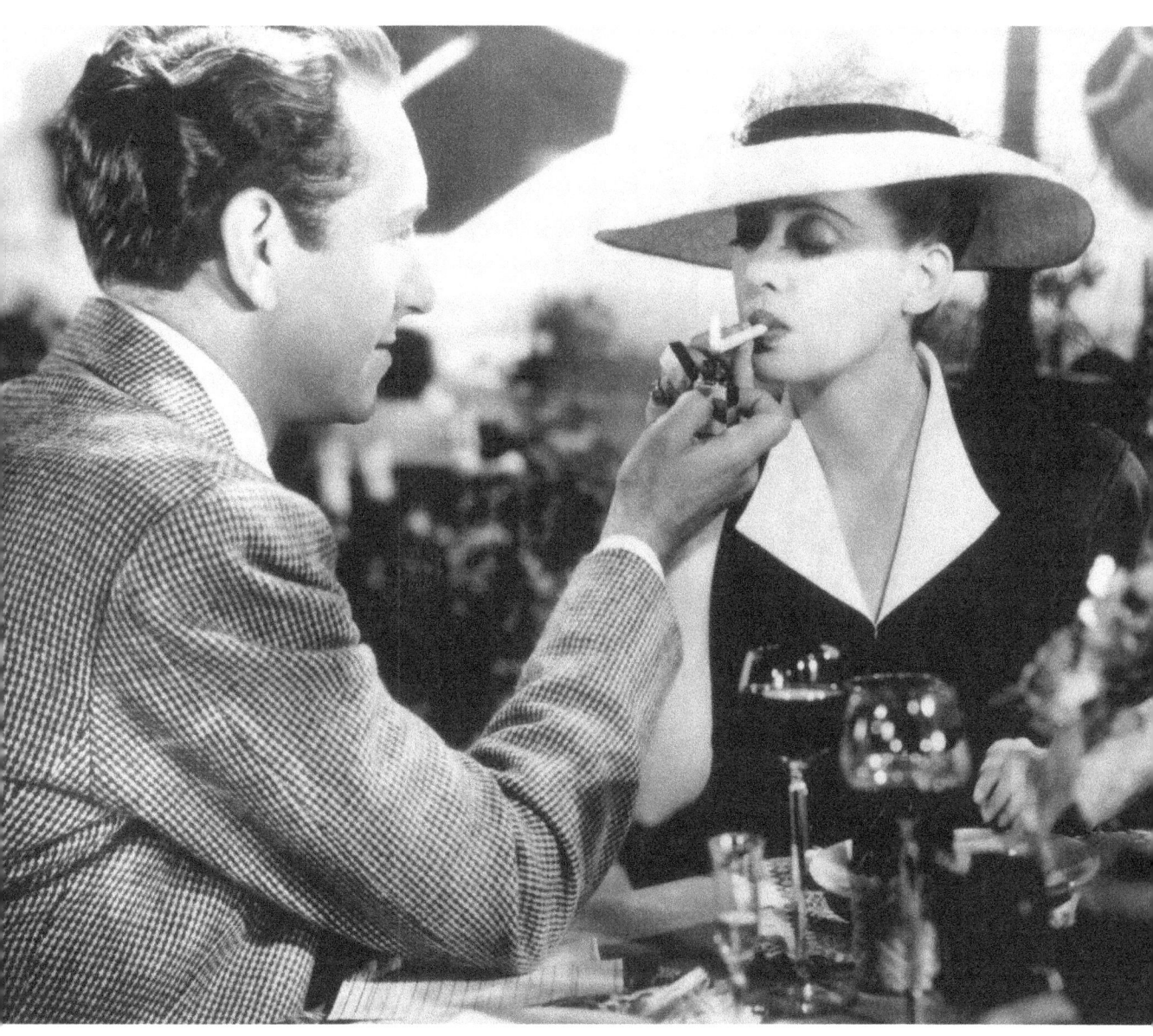

Bette Davis, in *Now Voyage*;; the best makeover film.

CHAPTER 15
REALLY!

"Lack of self-worth is the fundamental source of all emotional pain.
A feeling of insecurity, unworthiness and lack of value
is the core experience of powerlessness."

~ Gary Zukav and Linda Francis from *The Heart of the Soul*

I wear my hair very short. I can shower, blow dry my hair, put on my makeup in fifteen minutes or less. To me short hair is freedom. I suspect Joan of Arc must have been exhilarated by that fact when she cut her hair. Of course she wanted to fight for France but I'm not sure gender equality wasn't the true motive for her call for freedom. In spite of her efforts the royals of the day executed her anyway. They didn't like her politics or her haircut.

As an instructor of Cosmetology every day on the clinic floor, I met women who admired my haircut; but they were afraid to try it. The excuse they always used was, their husband or the significant male in their life loved their hair long and they did not want them to cut or change it. They were wearing their hair long to please the male in their lives. I have seen women way past their prime carting around tons of hair they were still wearing as they did in high school. Believe me, by the way they looked, they were not doing themselves a favor.

What are these men saying to their wives or lovers? I won't love you as much if you get a haircut. You are a projection of my female fantasy and a woman must wear her hair long in the bedroom. Really?

The real question here is, "Whose hair is it?"

There are religious countries in the world where the male patriarchy is in charge of women's hair. They must cover their hair and exposing their asset would be dangerous for them not to obey. Are we being weighed down by the same oppression? Is the male standard of the female ideal still a measure of our worth and value? We are working women raising families. This is a standard that does not serve us anymore. Can we please break the bonds of male domination and cut our hair and still remain beautiful and sexy.

I get that women want the males in their lives to admire them. I understand that to keep their men from straying they have to compete with unrealistic images projected in the movies and television and the magazines. What I don't get, have they not seen...

Halle Berry, the ultimate Bond girl in *Die another Day,* the 2002 film, emerging from the ocean a goddess rising as Botticelli's *Venus.* Another short haired Bond Beauty is Carey Lowell in *License to Kill.*

The incomparable Charlize Theron, at the award ceremonies in her "show stopping" haircuts; the less hair she has the more fabulous she looks.

Demi Moore in *Ghost,* the 1990 film her hair was cut short looking sexy beautiful and vulnerable. I always hoped she would go back to the former look.

Audrey Hepburn getting her long hair cut was a supreme moment in the movie *Sabrina.* Elizabeth Taylor was exquisite in the *Last time I Saw Paris.* She cut her hair in the middle of the film and was more gorgeous in the second half than she was in the first if that was possible.

Kim Novak the blond iconic sex symbol wore her hair very short; actually when she let her hair get longer, she lost some of her uniqueness and appeal. In the 1985 movie *Year of the Dragon,* Arianne Koizumi plays Tracy Tzu, a television reporter. Her short haircut in the movie is just stunning. I always watch the film just to see her hair.

Today do we all have to look like the Kardashian sisters and wear our hair long? Is it possible to admire women who do not always have to wear extensions, or have a stylist, makeup artists, hair stylists and plastic surgeons as accessories? The new reality *celebrity housewives* are they the new role models for us to follow? They drink so much wine on these reality shows, I feel drunk watching them, and wake up with a hangover.

Let's celebrate the real women I see every day; the ones who represent who we really are. The women, who work hard for their families get up each day and make breakfast then lunches for their children, sort and start the laundry, make the beds and then go to work to the job that pays. They are single moms, and married, working moms. They clean their houses go to the grocery store, cook the meals help with homework, help with aged parent, squeeze in doctor and dentist appointments, go to their children's soccer games, keep up with friends and pay the bills. When is there time for the blow dry?

I'm not against long beautiful, lustrous hair. What I am for is choice in all areas of our life. I want us to have choice over our bodies and that includes our hair. I don't want a male dominated patriarchy to make the choices for me. Our bodies and images are ours not theirs to project judgments or idealized archetypes'.

Shakespeare's tragedy of *Hamlet* written in 1601—"This above all: To thine own self be true." Amazing how we need these words more today. Is this not the true essence of beauty, being true to oneself; living authentically and not as someone else's version of who we should be? Can we please be sexy with short hair if that is how we choose to wear it?

How does Shakespeare s message relate to us today? "To thine own self be true," and what does "authentic self" really mean?

It means to start listening to your heart and your inner voice more. Following your own concepts and ideas even if you're at the risk of being unpopular and the road gets too difficult. Not to be swayed by the media's false values. Listening to your truth is the essence of your soul speaking.

Finding your own individual style takes time, and practice on the road to discovering how to be whole and comfortable with yourself. It's amazing how complete you will become and how much better you will look in the mirror. The inside you and the outside you begin to balance.

If the haircut you're wearing is not the one you really want to wear but other people in your life like it on you…. change it. If you have the heart of a blond and you're a brunette…. go blond. If your husband loves you being a redhead and you don't...change it.

Try to follow your intuition more. That nagging still small voice you often avoid is right more frequently than not and is your truest friend. That voice is your authentic self-helping you to be more whole.

Loving your self is your best beauty asset and it's one we can afford. It cannot be bought in stores or found in a jar, bottle or a magazine advertisement. Confidence is sexy and the most desirable quality a woman can have.

Being honest and true to oneself is the one true anti-ageing serum that is timeless. Who knew that Shakespeare was the beauty expert extraordinaire yet he understood that knowing your own truth and living that truth is the real essence of beauty. That is the cosmetic treatment that endures.

Imagine a jar labeled and sold in stores as a repair serum called "Truth" as a beauty preparation. I wonder how that label would sell in the marketplace.

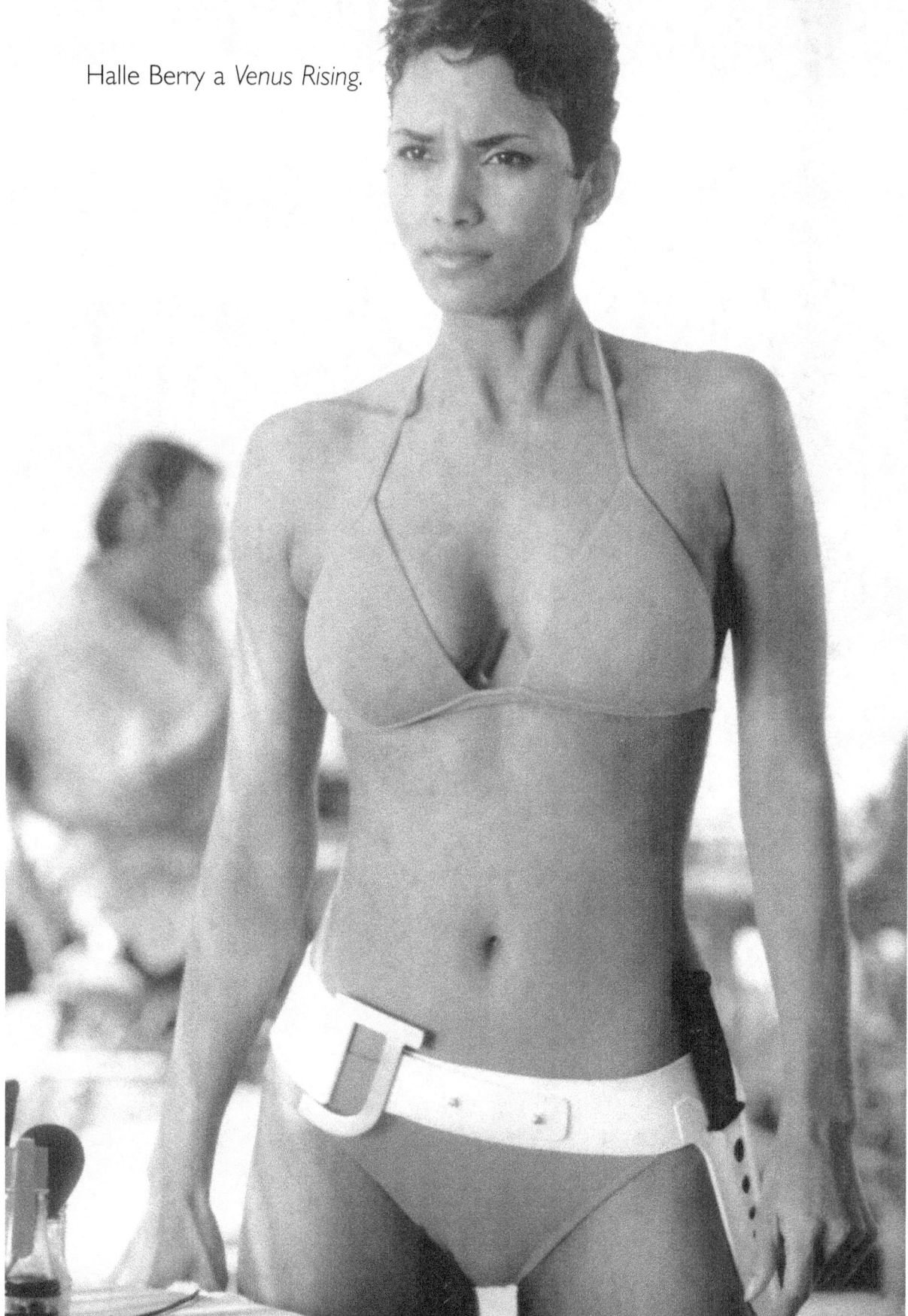

Halle Berry a *Venus Rising*.

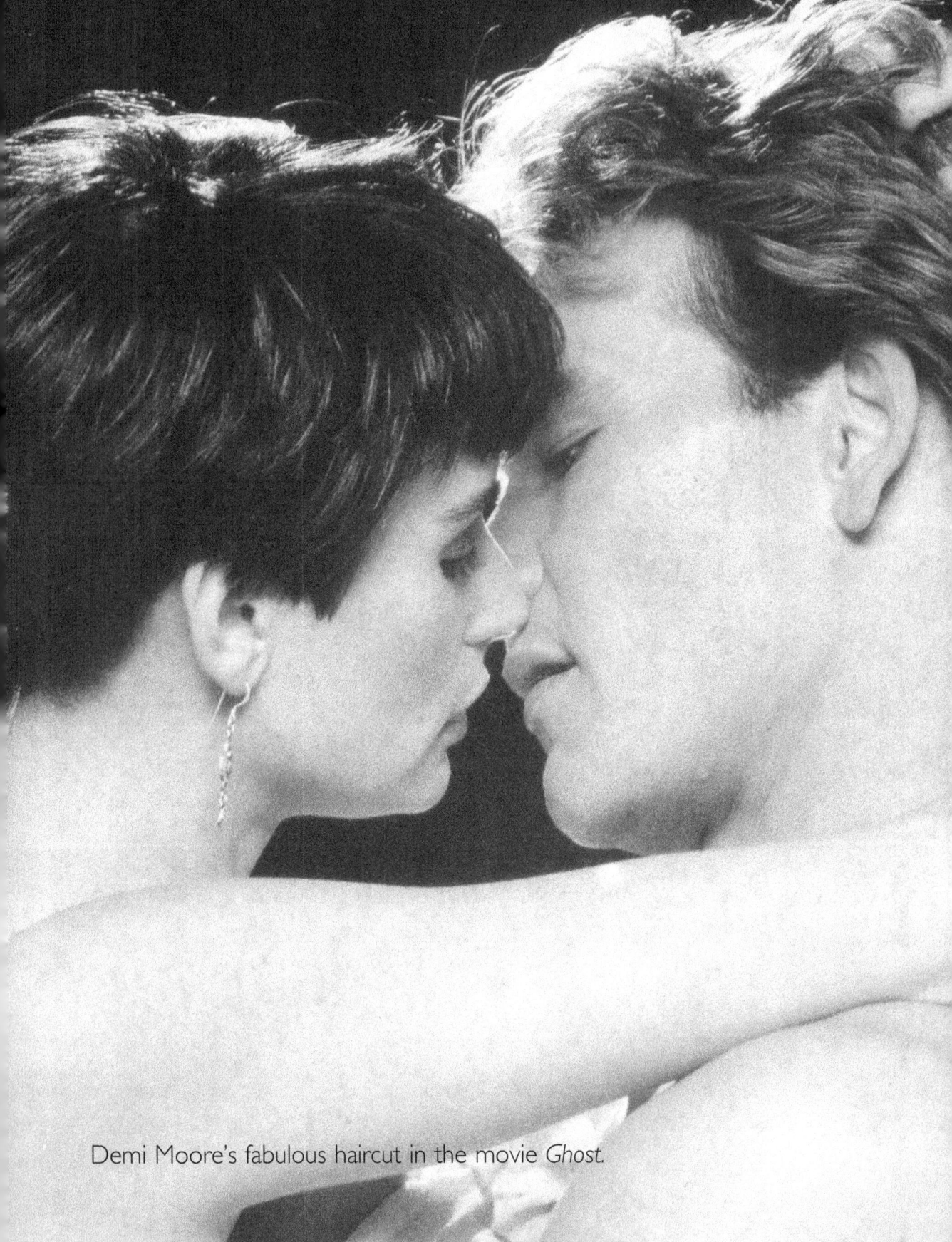

Demi Moore's fabulous haircut in the movie *Ghost*.

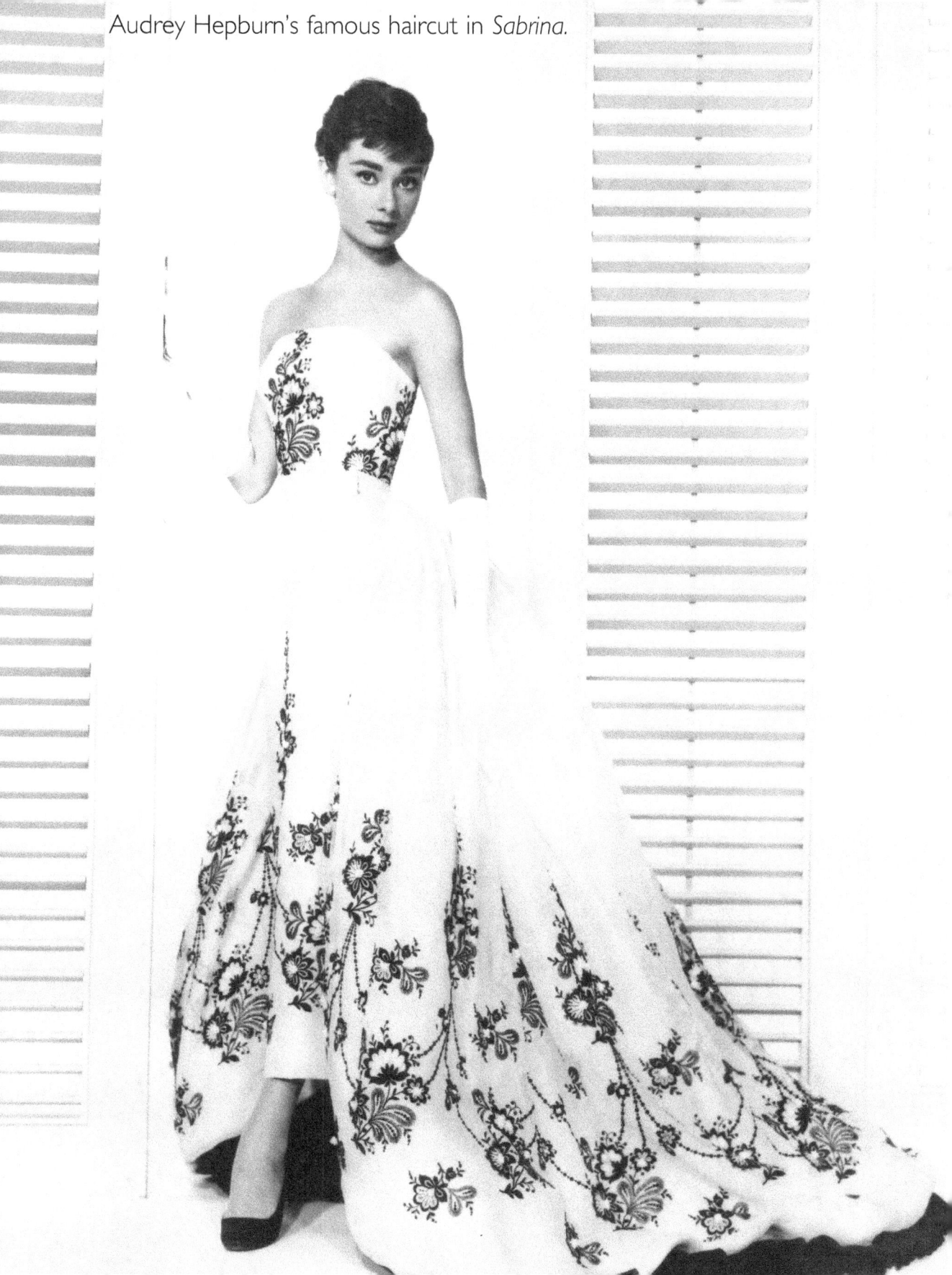

Audrey Hepburn's famous haircut in *Sabrina*.

CHAPTER 16
HAIR IS A SPIRITUAL JOURNEY

"No, you can't always get what you want
aaaahhwaw
No, you can't always get what you want
aaaahhwaw
No, you can't always get what you want
aaaahhwaw
But if you try sometime, you just might find
you get what you need."

Mick Jagger and Keith Richards

The earliest recollections of my hair have been a major determiner of how I felt about myself. I've had great hair days when I was amazed at how great it looked, and then I have also experienced bad hair years. Like the Greek deities of the old Greek myths I believed there was a hair God that I would secretly pray to.

Every day my hair surprised me. How my hair would perform and how it would look in the morning mirror? I knew that no matter how hard I tried I was not in control my hair was always in charge. Like everything in life there are lessons to be learned. Painful as they might be, Hair was going to be one of them. In fact hair can be a major teacher in our lifetime.

One of my earliest lessons was that hair has a language that speaks to us.

You really have to listen and pay attention to what your hair is saying to you. We are in a constant search for perfection, which always eludes us because we are never satisfied with the results of our search. The goal post always moves so the end result is never achieved. We may be happy for a short time but the happiness is not lasting it is temporary. Our hair sometimes suffers from our desire to change it so much, often putting it at risk.

The chemicals we use on our hair are strong and if not used carefully and without knowledge can cause severe damage. A lot of people do things that diminish the integrity of their hair and cause serious damage to it. Here is a compilation of some of the things we do to our hair. Is any of this familiar to you?

- You want to change your black hair that you changed two weeks ago. Now you want to be a lighter blond perhaps platinum as the goal. You tried doing it yourself the night before from the box of color sold at the drugstore and now your hair is bright orange.

- Today you're tired of being a blond and you want to go back to your original brown hair and the fine texture of your hair is really fragile. You were told to wait and get your hair a little healthier but you want it done now.

- You just did highlights in your hair, but you want to be blonder and bolder. Or you think the highlights should be much darker and now after its darker it is too dark and now you want the highlights lighter again.

- Or maybe instead of the blond highlights you want them to be red. A few weeks later you hate the red and you want to go back to the blond; and the ends of your hair are beginning to look a little fried.

- You are a freshly done platinum blond and you want your hair with more curl from a perm; or the freshly done highlights wants less curl and straighter strands with a relaxer. The results of both services would be dangerous for your hair.

- The curly hair has had too many relaxers. The straight hair client has had too many perms either might result in breakage and hair loss.

- You love to wear your hair long and cutting the split ends is simply not an option. So you would rather sacrifice the health of your hair in favor of keeping the length and not cut the split ends off.

- Finally you realize it might be better for your hair to cut the split ends but it must not affect the   length of your hair. So you only cut it an eighth of an inch and the split ends go half way up the hair strand.

- You loved your new short haircut but now you're unhappy and want your long hair back. Is there something the stylist can do? How about a magic wand instead of a comb?

- A lot of people want the new colors: purple, pink, blue, green and teal. It requires a lot of maintenance to insure against the fading of these colors but you don't want to invest in the time or trouble and money.

- A layered cut was asked for, but in the last six weeks you hate it and want a style without the layers. Can I make it one length again?

- Should you cover the gray or not cover the gray? So you decided to cover the gray and after the gray was covered you feel the hair is too dark for your face and now you want to go back to the original gray.

After all the things you have done to your hair were you respectful of the relationship and did you really listen to what your hair was saying to you? Did you stop paying attention to the warnings and the signs, the split ends, the breakage and the lack of luster? Were you so self-absorbed that you ignored the stress and suffering you were putting your hair through?

When your hair was crying for a better shampoo and conditioning treatments did you disregard what it was trying to tell you. Did you buy the cheapest shampoo on the shelf and forget to use the conditioner? Did you overdose on color and neglect to heed what the professionals were saying? Was keeping the length of your hair more important than cutting off the damaged split ends? Was breakage and separation from the scalp the only option left for your hair? Did you have to lose your hair before really listening to what it had to say?

Hair is our teacher and teaches us lessons no matter how painful they are. Like most of life we learn our lessons through painful mistakes and hopefully get to enlightenment. When hair is valued and taken care of it is alive and pulsating with vibrancy and energy. Like everything in life, when it is carefully nurtured it radiates happiness.

Can we learn to surrender and accept the heredity we were born with? Can we love the color of the roots of our ancestors? Can we accept our hairs texture and accept the straight hair that won't hold a curl, as well as love the waves and extra curly hair we were not born with? Can we love and accept the thin strands and not wish they were thicker? Is it possible to love our fatter hair and not long for our strands to be thinner?

Can we embrace and celebrate the differences in our hair and be less critical? Hair the wise teacher tells us to accept are true selves and deeply love our authenticity. Is it possible to honor and care for our hair no matter what the season, and in the ageing process love and honor our hairs winter?

There are many ways in our culture we can define beauty. We must adhere to a deeper inner beauty as the standard to strive for, because style and fashion are fickle and intangible. Popular culture tells us what the ideals of beauty should be via television, magazines, movies and music. Is it possible to transcend the media and have our own criteria of what is beautiful? Most importantly, the media is and always will be in the business that is driven by profit.

Might we consider the internal attributes as a measure of what is beautiful and be kinder in the judgments we so critically place on ourselves? Kindness, compassion, and generosity of spirit are also elements of being beautiful.

Over the years I have been witness to how illness and chemotherapy can ravage a women's hair. The vision of what their hair used to be is a dimmed memory. The bravery and courage of these women continuing to live without their hair was a badge of valor they symbolically wore when they had stood at life's edge. These women raise the bar and are examples of what true beauty is, and they are a new standard for women to admire. Their hair tells the story of great strength and true grit and they are the real heroines of todays' beauty.

I believe John Keats, the romantic poet said it best in 1820 in his poem, *Ode to A Grecian Urn*:

> "Beauty is truth, truth beauty
> That is all... Ye know on earth, and all ye need to know"

CHAPTER 17
THE POWER OF HAIR

"I want long, straight, curly, fuzzy, snaggy, shaggy, ratty, matty
Oily, greasy, fleecy, shining, gleaming, streaming, flaxen, waxen
Knotted, polka dotted, twisted, beaded, braided
Powered, flowered and confettied
Bangled, tangled, spangled and spaghettied"

Hair, the musical sound track
James Rado, Gait MacDermot, Gerome Ragni

What is it about our hair that has such a profound influence on our well-being? Why do we spend so much money and time obsessing about those grand strands of protein emanating from the crown of our heads? No matter how young we are or how old we get, our hair has a powerful impact on us. It has the capacity to thrill and excite and also cause us distress when we are looking at our reflected image in the mirror.

   If you had decided not to wash your hair because you were running late or just too tired, you would probably suffer all day, and be sorry that you didn't wash it earlier that morning. You wouldn't feel good until your head was under a faucet bubbling with shampoo and rinsed with water. If you are in need of a root touch- up or a haircut, you would agonize waiting until the appointment was scheduled and the service completed. Then afterwards be ecstatic with the results. Hair can make your day, boost your confidence and actually make you feel better.

   A haircut can change and enhance your mood by the time you are at blow- dry. Covering the regrowth or changing the color can bring happiness in less than two hours; that is hair's power. I don't know of one anti-depressant drug that can work that fast and produce results as quickly and effectively without ghastly side effects. How we look and how we feel are directly related and our emotions echo that phenomenon. After giving hundreds of haircuts, I am convinced it affects us on a cellular level. Hair is anything but dead it's alive and well and hopefully, thriving on your head.

When I was a young girl, hair would always be what I would first notice about someone walking down the street. In high school, I would make judgments about a boy by how he styled his hair. If he had great hair, I would immediately be drawn to him without even knowing if he were nice and of course the opposite was true as well. A serial killer might have gotten a pass from me if he had a great haircut!

When I am in a grocery store, I will follow a great haircut up and down the aisles just to get a better glimpse of it from the front and the back. Hair usually grows a half inch a month and I have spent years waiting for an unflattering haircut to grow out. Decades have been spent financing those remarkable strands. I always knew my hair mattered, I just really didn't understand why it mattered so much. Sixty years later, I now know …

Hair matters because hair is art. Hair is the canvas for the expression of our creativity. Hair is art and cosmetologists are artists. They artfully design and style the hair that surround and frame our faces. Make up and fashion are also part of the artistry We are the creators of our own designs made from the choices and inspirations that surround us every day. How we put it all together is the real task of the artist and that is where the true talent lies.

This is why when we sit in airports, restaurants and cafes we are always looking at each other. We can't stop staring, gaping and gawking because we are just so interesting to watch and we never tire of this sport. "People watching" is our favorite international pastime loved by everyone around the world. Our curiosity is the real fuel that creates the genuine power for the celebrities. We love to observe and analyze their hair, makeup and what they are wearing. They inspire our own creativity and give us the courage to invent ourselves and have fun in the process.

We are "art-walking" down the street having coffee at Starbucks or standing at the bus stop on our way to work. We are a virtual parade of the ideas, trends and current street art put forth by the choices we make each day. There is no cost to enjoy the show, if we have the mind- set to view it from an artistic perspective .

Throughout history we have always decorated our hair and bodies to express creativity and how we felt about ourselves. According to the British Broadcasting Corporation in 2003, an excavation in Amesbury at Wiltshire, England found a body of a man from 3500 B C who had gold ornaments in his hair.

Cleopatra knew the power of a hair style and makeup. Trendsetter extraordinaire she set herself apart from everyone else. Her hair and eyeliner brought down an empire and Caesar and Mark Antony along with it.

Samson from the Bible, a true rock star understood hairs power. He loved to wear his hair long. Along came shady Delilah and cut his hair while he was sleeping. Samson woke up furious and brought the whole house down. I guess he didn't like the cut and you could bet he did not rebook with Delilah again. Was she just doing a makeover on Samson or trying to cut off his power. And you know what they say about strong women?

Hair is Art and it follows the rules of line, balance, order and color just as a painting or a sculpture. We must recognize and appreciate this art form and not judge it too harshly. That would be a great misunderstanding because the art exists to delight and make us ponder the experience.

There is another song from the sixtie's Broadway play, *Hair*: "Let the sunshine, let the sun shine in." My song to you is, "Let the art shine, let the art shine in." Living in the technological age we do, I fervently hope that art does not get lost. I pray there is always a place for the artists in our society. They are the life force of a society and a mirror for every decade. The artist always tells the story in ways that history doesn't. Art and the artist are the representatives of a culture's truth.

Charles Dickens book, *A Christmas Carol*, written in 1843 endures as a story. It was originally written to tell the story of a Christmas in London. It has now morphed into an American Christmas classic. Every season since 1843 it has been a staple of our holiday tradition.

Jane Austen is more popular now than she was in 1811. Tolstoy and other great philosophers' ideas and visions have lasted through centuries. Art and ideas are impervious to time. The creative dream of an artist can have the power to influence and inspire.

Our hair matters because it is the outer expression of who we are and how we want to be perceived. It is a large part of our own story and our stories and hair change as we do. Hair manifests itself and changes from our birth to old age and serves as a metaphor for our life's history and denotes where we are in it's timeline. Hair is art, a practice and a ritual that symbolizes we are here.

RESOURCE INDEX ACKNOWLEDGEMENTS

Chapters and Pictures:

Chapter I: A Place of Their Own: The Fifties
    Kim Novak—*Vertigo*

Chapter III: Revenge of the Hair Mummies
    A Summer Place — Sandra Dee and Troy Donahue
    George Hamilton
    The Beatles, Joan Baez

Chapter IV: The Sasson
    Annette Funnicello (Big Hair)

Chapter V: The Wedding Album
    Author's Wedding Pictures

Chapter VI: The Sixties
    Inauguration Snapshots of Jack and Jackie Kennedy

Chapter VII: The Seventies
    Coming Home – Jane Fonda and John Voight

Chapter VIII: The Eighties and Ninties
    Charlie's Angels
    Dynasty Stars
    Madonna

About the Author

Elayne Becker holds a graduate degree in Fine Arts. She had a thirty year career as an interior designer in the San francisco Bay Area. Her work has been featured numerous times in *Better Homes and Gardens, Homes and Design* and *HGTV Homes of San Francisco*.

Ms. Becker started a second career at age of sixty two. She graduated from the the Paul Mitchell School and became an educator of cosmetology. She now teaches at the J.D. Academy in Danville, California and designs hair styles for private clients.

ABOOKS

ALIVE Books, ALIVE Book Publishing and
ALIVE Publishing Group are imprints of
Advanced Publishing LLC,
3200 A Danville Blvd., Suite 204, Alamo, California 94507

Telephone: 925.837.7303 Fax: 925.837.6951
www.alivebookpublishing.com

www.ingramcontent.com/pod-product-compliance
Lightning Source LLC
Chambersburg PA
CBHW081148280526
45787CB00008B/3251